LETTERS *from a* COUNSELOR

Christmas and Holy Week
Messages to Missionaries
from Pastor Wayne Schulz

LETTERS *from a* COUNSELOR

Christmas and Holy Week
Messages to Missionaries
from Pastor Wayne Schulz

All Scripture quotations, unless otherwise indicated, are taken from the HOLY BIBLE, NEW INTERNATIONAL VERSION®, NIV®. Copyright © 1973, 1978, 1984 by Biblica, Inc.™ Used by permission of Zondervan. All rights reserved worldwide.

All rights reserved. No part of this publication may be reproduced, stored in a retrieval system, or transmitted in any form or by any means—electronic, mechanical, photocopying, recording, or otherwise—except for brief quotations in reviews, without prior permission of the author or the editor.

Joel A. Schulz, editor
3964 Beacham Street, Mississauga, ON, Canada
joel.schulz@crossoflife.net
905-785-6765

© 2013 Wayne I. Schulz
Published 2013

Printed in the United States of America by
Morris Publishing®
3212 East Highway 30
Kearney, NE 68847
1-800-650-7888

ISBN 978-0-615-72846-9
Library of Congress Control Number 2013900762

Cover image: iStockphoto.com
Cover design by Joel A. Schulz

This book is dedicated
above all to Jesus Christ,
whose incarnation, cross, and empty tomb
changed Wayne's life forever.

It is also dedicated to Anita,
Wayne's loving wife,
who faithfully served the Lord
alongside Wayne throughout his ministry.
He loved her dearly.

CONTENTS

Foreword		9
Christmas 1997	The Image Smasher	13
Holy Week 1998	Blessed Is He	17
Christmas 1998	Greetings in the Christ Child	23
Holy Week 1999	*Missing*	27
Christmas 1999	Fear and Death and Sorrow Cease	29
Holy Week 2000	Holy Tuesday	33
Christmas 2000	The Light Shines	37
Holy Week 2001	Death and Taxes, Bach and BIC	41
Christmas 2001	The Real Lord of the Rings!	47
Holy Week 2002	Clop, Clop, Clop	51
Christmas 2002	O Light Divine!	57
Holy Week 2003	It's Not What One Would Think	61
Christmas 2003	And the Desert Shall Rejoice	67
Holy Week 2004	Do Not Weep!	73
Christmas 2004	God Is with Us	77
Holy Week 2005	The Lord Needs A Donkey	83
Christmas 2005	Christus Paradox in the Manger	89
Holy Week 2006	Oh, and Jesus Didn't Die on the Cross?	95
Christmas 2006	Grinch	101
Holy Week 2007	Attitude	109
Christmas 2007	Christ to the World with Joy We Bring	115
Holy Week 2008	St. Patrick and Holy Week 2008	121
Christmas 2008	When's It Going To Happen?	125
Holy Week 2009	What Shall I Do with Christ?	131
Christmas 2009	Your Life Is Not Insignificant	135
Holy Week 2010	Easter Words	141
Christmas 2010	Bold in the Faith	147
Holy Week 2011	Rejoicing in the Resurrection Grave	153
Afterword		161
Notes		165

FOREWORD

Every Christmas and Holy Week, the gospel-driven, mission-minded people whom Pastor Wayne Schulz served as WELS Mission Counselor would receive a letter in their Inboxes. It would momentarily take them out of the whirlwind of preparations for the upcoming season of gospel outreach and draw them into the presence of God.

The letter was the result of digging deeply into the Word and came from a heart fired up by the Holy Spirit that wanted more than anything else to share the good news of our Savior with the lost. A heart that wanted more than anything to give the hope of Jesus to the hopeless. A ministry dedicated to inspiring, empowering, and encouraging his colleagues to step out into the world and share the gospel with all people.

These letters may have started coming by postal mail, but in 1997 they began arriving via "new-fangled" e-mail and the distribution list grew quickly. Though the letters were delivered in different ways over the years, their origin was always the same: Dad, sitting at his computer with his Bible open on his desk, enjoying a midwinter's snowy scene outside his window, and Handel's *Messiah* or a Bach cantata playing in the background.

As a missionary myself, the moment one of these letters arrived in my Inbox (sometimes my dad even gave me a preview), I would take an uncharacteristic break, maybe put on the *Messiah* as well, and immerse myself in the encouraging words. In my home mission, Christmas and Holy Week are always tremendously busy times in which we do all we can to get the gospel message out to the people of our community. These times are often fraught with frustrations and hardships as we prepare. So every time I received one of these "letters from a counselor," it was exactly what I needed to hear and reminded me why what we were doing to share Jesus was so important. Each letter lifted me up with God's powerful Word.

But Wayne Schulz was really speaking in behalf of the lost. The reason he wrote these letters to his missionaries during these crucial times was to spur them on to action and encourage them to do what is necessary to reach the lost with the gospel of Jesus. On the day Ed Schuppe was installed as mission counselor, he looked to Wayne for mentoring. He asked him, "What is the most important role of a mission counselor?" Wayne answered: *"The role of the mission counselor is to be the voice of the unchurched in every one of our congregations."*

FOREWORD

So let these letters be that for you. For your church. For your leadership team. For your family. Let them be the voice of the unchurched in your congregation. Let them remind you of the urgent task you have to reach the lost with the gospel of Jesus.

I haven't changed or edited them very much. I hope you find them mostly as they were sent. You will notice some of the first ones are a bit more informal. One even gives an update on our family. As they go along, they dig to deeper depths and push to greater urgency in sharing the gospel. My prayer for you, as you read them, is that you are lifted up with God's grace and encouraged in your role of reaching the lost with Jesus.

My father was never one to seek praise or recognition. He wanted that to go to his Lord and Savior. So here is the best part about these brief letters: You are not going to read them and find yourself thinking, "Wayne Schulz was so great." You are going to read these letters and find yourself proclaiming, "Our Lord is so great!"

In Jesus' Name,
Joel Schulz, Wayne's son
October 8, 2012

CHRISTMAS 1997

THE IMAGE SMASHER

Dear friends in missions and friends of missions! What a privilege all of us have—to advance the message of Immanuel during this Christmas season! With faith's certainty we can say and sing and shout that Jesus is "God with us." A French Christmas carol describes the Incarnation this way: "Supreme royalty has put on a slave's dress." This is one of those deep Gospel mysteries that brings joy and delight when it is proclaimed and explained.

Missionary Mark Paustian, Rockford, IL, writes about this Immanuel in *Forward in Christ* magazine. There he calls him the "Iconoclast," the Image Smasher. Permit me to share some of his thoughts.

Jesus came into the world to shatter every false idea about who God is and to show us the truth. "The Son is the radiance of God's glory, the exact representation of his being" (Hebrews 1:3). Jesus came into the world to reveal to you and to me exactly who God is.

Since sin began, human beings have fashioned God in their own image: from Greek and Roman mythical gods...to our own culture's false god (whose biggest concern seems to be that we're all enjoying ourselves—God as tolerant grandfather). There is the do-nothing god, who may or may not exist.... Or we imagine him as a "Force," as impersonal and unfeeling as a jolt of electricity. Maybe we make him the Cosmic Bookkeeper, who likes nothing better than to catch us in a sin (and then gets even by stalling our car...in the middle of State St.). Or he is the...mere idea to be debated and then filed away.... It's all the same. Caricatures and lies.

But thank God for God! As you think of all the false images of the One-who-made-us...[there] stands Jesus. God-made-known, real, alive, in flesh and blood.

The image smasher.

The iconoclast.

The radiance of God's glory.

The Image Smasher

The exact representation of God's being.

The One who came to demolish every wrong idea of who God is. "No one has ever seen God, but God the One and Only, who is at the Father's side, has made him known" (John 1:18).

This Christmas, watch the Image Smasher being born in a stable. See his hand wrapped around Joseph's thumb…caressing the face of the leper…clawing the ground of Gethsemane…cruelly nailed to the wood. Watch him take his first steps…to the cross. Draw close to the one who would rather die than live without you. And you know who God is.[1]

Thank you for these thoughts, Mark! They overpowered the flippant remarks I heard on the radio while driving from Milwaukee this morning: "A Merry Christmas to all of you! And to you atheists, have a nice day." Aren't you glad you are in the business of Gospel proclamation?

This Christmas I thank God that you are part of Immanuel's team! Anita joins me in wishing all of you a blessed Christmas and another year of service for Christ!

Wayne Schulz
Christmas 1997

Holy Week 1998

Blessed Is He

"Blessed is he who comes in the name of the Lord!" (Matthew 21:9).

It's called green space, and it's right behind our lot. Sounds nice. Actually, it's a place where huge weeds compete with wild raspberry branches to suffocate six pine trees. Trying to save the pines, I began to whack the weeds. Soon the raspberry branches were doing their best to make the task miserable.

Those prickly branches reminded me of the crown of thorns folded and forced on the head of Jesus. Suddenly my self-pity disappeared. Thoughts went to him, God made flesh, him who became obedient to death—even death on a cross.

Letters from a Counselor

What a scene to contemplate this week!

History's most holy week began with the whole crowd of disciples joyfully praising God: "Blessed is the king who comes in the name of the Lord! Peace in heaven and glory in the highest!" That's about all the Pharisees could take. "Rebuke your disciples!" they told Jesus.

"I tell you," he replied, "if they keep quiet, the stones will cry out" (Luke 19:38-40). Soon there would be quieting of acclamation. Soon there would be forsaking and flight. Soon there would be dying and death. "At that moment the curtain of the temple was torn in two from top to bottom. The earth shook and the rocks split" (Matthew 27:51). An untimely coincidence? A chance happening? Hardly.

There may be growing temptations from outside of you and inside of you to quiet acclamation, to abandon proclamation. Will that stop you? Hardly! You know that the crown of thorns and the grave were not the end. You know that God exalted Jesus to the highest place. You know that his name is above every name. You know that "at the name of Jesus every knee should bow... and every tongue confess that Jesus Christ is Lord, to the glory of God the Father" (Philippians 2:10,11). What a difference that has made!

Keep quiet? Not a chance! Not this week.

Not ever.

AN EXPERIMENT

It is experimental for me to send this to you via e-mail. There are about 100 of you on my mailing list. Since you would not care to read two pages worth of addresses, I am sending this to little batches of you at a time. If I do not have your e-mail address, I will send you this the slow way. That's a gentle hint to you to get me your e-mail address! I think e-mail can save me some time. And perhaps I can do even more of these!

PLANNING

After Easter, most of you will be getting serious about doing your annual planning. Remember that solid churches are not built in a day. God can build a mushroom in a short period of time, less than a day. But he takes years to build a strong oak tree. In Isaiah 61 he calls people his "oaks of righteousness." There are no shortcuts in this growing process.

As you plan, clarify the purpose for everything you do. Ask, "How does this fit in with what God expects us to be doing? With our mission statement? What are the vital issues of our congregation as it strives to bring God's Word to the people of this community?" If something does not fall under this purpose, why do it? Focus on the essentials. Keep it simple. Learn from mistakes. Build from your strengths. Let your members understand and appreciate your congregation's strengths. Let them grow in asking, "What can we do to show the unchurched not only that Christ *is* the answer but also *how* he is the answer to their needs, their deepest questions, their sins?" People are interested in biblical doctrine when it is applied in practical ways to their lives.

Consider, for instance, *Christian education.* Could I guess that this often comes up somewhat short in your [ministry] planning? There really is no excuse for hit-and-miss "What would you like to study next?" planning in 1998. Work on a core curriculum. There is the *Adult Bible Study Handbook* (three-ringed binder) from the Board for Parish Services. Research also the increasing number of courses available from NPH.

Head knowledge (who, what, when, how) is a purpose of a Bible class. However, it is not the only purpose. Many classes get bogged down at this place, I feel. The vital points may be overlooked.

Heart knowledge is another purpose of a Bible class. What do all these objective facts of Christ mean for the world? For me? God chose me to be his disciple! His work has made a difference for me! I'm part of the holy Christian Church!

Lifestyle/Witness knowledge also needs to be stressed. How can this lesson be applied to my life, my alien life in this world? How can this lesson build up mission-mindedness? At times it may be good to have a *planned* lull (two weeks?) between courses so that growing Christians can practice what they have learned (before they file it away). Maybe a planned activity with time to return, review, and report to the group? "Do not merely listen to the word, and so deceive yourselves. Do what it says" (James 1:22). Incidentally, Mission Counselor John Huebner has written an extensive course on lifestyle witnessing. It will be featured in one of the next issues of *Mission Connection*. Possibly (!) it may be made available on a computer disk. Christian education and witness go hand in hand with worship, fellowship, and stewardship.

> In Christ,
> Wayne Schulz
> April 5, 1998

Christmas 1998

Greetings in the Christ Child

Greetings in the name of the Christ Child to all my friends who work in the Lord's mission!

At the end of another year, I pray that you will reflect and make your own some of the thoughts I am gleaning from an American Christmas carol anonymously published in New Hampshire in 1784 called "Jesus Christ the Apple Tree." In its own way, it speaks to the heart and reflects thoughts that go through the minds of all people, even the restless and searching unchurched. St. Augustine said that the soul is not at rest until it finds its rest in God.

> "The Tree of Life my soul hath seen,
> Laden with fruit, and always green.
> The trees of nature fruitless be
> Compared with Christ the Apple Tree."

Letters from a Counselor

You in the mission fields are rest-bringers and rest-givers! You who have eaten from the Tree of Life have also taken that food to nourish souls in 1998, many who previously have tasted the dead trees of nature and society and have come away empty. Only Christ fills the hungry with good things!

> **"For happiness I long have sought,**
> **And pleasures dearly I have bought;**
> **I missed of all; but now I see**
> **'Tis found in Christ the Apple Tree.**
>
> **"This fruit doth make my soul to thrive,**
> **It keeps my dying faith alive;**
> **Which makes my soul in haste to be**
> **With Jesus Christ the Apple Tree."**

What a privilege to be bringers of this good news to the seekers! On a journey they are, searching for something that gives meaning, that puts it all together, longing for happiness that is not frivolous or fleeting or pseudo or giddy—for many, a journey to nowhere. But Christ the Apple Tree comes, probably through the message of your voice, in your demeanor, in your concern, and in your servant spirit, all of which say, "Here! Hurry to the Apple Tree! Come! Eat! Here is food for the soul, food that removes the hunger of your painful life. Here! Look nowhere else!"

Greetings in the Christ Child

"Did I really do this?" you may ask. "Is it all this simple?" Yes, Yes, Yes! All the knocking, all the printing, all the phoning, all the folding, all the mailing, all the teaching, all the preaching, all the pleading, all the praying, all the singing, all the sharing—all worth it. No doubt about it! Because the Apple Tree is growing in you, raising you up to let people taste and see and enjoy and be satisfied—eternally!

> **"I'm weary with my former toil;**
> **Here I will sit and rest a while,**
> **Under the shadow I will be,**
> **Of Jesus Christ the Apple Tree."**

Take some time with your loved ones. Rest a while next to the manger scene, bathed in the shadow from the cross. Listen carefully to the carols. Look to the light of the empty grave. Remember that your robes are washed and that you have a right to the glory which you now can see in Jesus Christ the Apple Tree.

I thank you for your work! There are more explorers than in any of my previous nine years as mission counselor. I thank you for your work! There are four mission boards out there who have a heart for the Lord and for the lost and for the missionaries. I thank you for your work! There are wives and families who share the mission vision and march along with the forward movement of the church!

Letters from a Counselor

If I do not have your e-mail address, please send it! It is a big time-saver on this end, and it permits me to stay in touch with you. Pardon the electronic way of sending this to most of you!

Let me know if you have interesting stories of how people have fed on Christ the Apple Tree. People want to hear from you through *Mission Connection*. It's a tool for you to use!

Anita joins me in wishing you special blessings this Christmas!

Wayne

Holy Week 1999

Missing

Christmas 1999

Fear and Death and Sorrow Cease

"Proclaim the birth of Christ and peace, that fear and death and sorrow cease" (Jaroslav Vajda, "Before the Marvel of This Night").

This may look like an annual report or a chronicle of our family's annual history at your expense! No matter how you view it, come along for the sleigh ride and join us in celebration of another year of God's grace, blessing, and opportunity to serve.

Anita continued her piano teaching at Holy Cross, Luther Preparatory School, and home. She limbered up her joints by directing Singers for Christ, a choral group from various congregations. She recovered beautifully from an automobile accident in February and turned to relaxing bike riding with me this fall. She accompanied me to the LWMS convention, the worship conference, and a School of Outreach in Tennessee—not to the synod convention in hot and humid New Ulm, however! Incidentally, our biking goal for 2000 is to get to London, little known London, that is, about seven miles east of here! Even my mission counselor itinerary does not quite get me to London yet!

Juliane and Jeremy are our primary guests during school breaks and summer vacations. In addition to long work hours, they work diligently at physical conditioning. Juliane continues her basketball, track, and music pursuits along with her studies at Martin Luther College, where she enjoys her roommate and a certain young man. Jeremy is in his last year at MLC before steering his silver Jetta to the seminary next fall. He and Juliane are forming a canvassing team for a trip to northern Alabama during spring break.

God used the month of May to help us determine our summer travel schedule. Jason graduated from Wisconsin Lutheran Seminary and, like his older brother, was assigned as tutor/instructor at Michigan Lutheran Seminary. Before his move, he and Nate Koelpin, Dawn's brother, traveled in Europe for about a month. On August 29, he was ordained, with his dad preaching the sermon. His Call Day gathering was at Mel and Eunice Heckendorf's place, where Grandma Schulz claims her origin.

Fear and Death and Sorrow Cease

Joel and Dawn made another Call Day appearance at the seminary. There they received the news that they would leave the USA and make their home in the greater Toronto area of Canada. They live in a spacious house in Oakville with the intent of starting a church in Mississauga, population 575,000, yet a mere suburb of Toronto. In spring they will move to Mississauga, and, God willing, welcome a child into their lives in June. Juliane, Jeremy, Jason, and Dawn's parents joined us for Joel's installation service. We were also privileged to see Toronto's sites and Niagara Falls.

While gathered around Janine's Easter table in Huntsville, Alabama, trying to become acquainted with Emma, granddaughter #1, Jim abruptly announced to all of us that Emma was going to have a little sibling come October. As promised, Evan James came into this world on October 9. Anita spent a week with Jim and Janine, and I made a quick trip for the baptism. Coupled with all of this, Jim's congregation decided to relocate. That meant the sale of all properties and a 23-mile move to Madison, Alabama. While this was taking place, a flood wiped out most of Jim's library, which was already packed in boxes for the move.

Jonathan made the MATC bookstore so efficient that they needed only one person to run it. He is now chief security officer of the First Bank Building, an all-glass building across the street from the capitol. There he sits in his black suit and welcomes all guests. If you are homeless, he will not permit you to sack out on the premises for a long period of time. In case Bonnie and Clyde show up, Jon will join you in running out of there as rapidly as possible!

Everyone will be with us the week after Christmas. That will be a treat! We will see to it that my parents from Beaver Dam join us for part of the time. If you are in our vicinity, please stop to visit.

May the blessings of the Christ Child accompany you into the new millennium!

Holy Week 2000

Holy Tuesday

On Tuesday, the 12th of Nisan, storm clouds of satanic opposition were ominously closing in on the holy Lamb of God. It was an exhausting day for Jesus in his last appearance in the temple. All day he had to fend off the verbal assaults of the Jewish leaders. First, it was the Pharisees with their sly question concerning the legality of giving tribute to Caesar. Next, the Sadducees posed their question about the widow with seven husbands in the final resurrection. Then the Pharisees tried again with their question about the greatest commandment in the Law.

In every instance, Jesus pointed out their shocking ignorance of God's Word and their misuse of his holy Law. In striving to keep the outward letter of the Law, they missed its entire inner spirit. Then in a series of thunderous "woes," Jesus scathingly denounced the rank hypocrisy of these "blind guides," this "brood of vipers."

This may be a good time to read Matthew 23 in its entirety to remember your own desperate need for the messages of Maundy Thursday, Good Friday, and Easter. Then one can preach and witness as one who has known the depths.

"O Jerusalem, Jerusalem, you who kill the prophets and stone those sent to you, how often I have longed to gather your children together, as a hen gathers her chicks under her wings, and you were not willing" (Matthew 23:37). Can you imagine everything that went through the mind of Jesus that Holy Tuesday? One is reminded of the Reproaches *(Improperia)* in the "Service of the Cross of Christ" for Good Friday:

"Thus says the Lord: What have I done to you, O my people, and wherein have I offended you? Answer me. What more could have been done for my vineyard than I have done for it? When I looked for good grapes, why did it yield only bad? My people, is this how you thank your God? O my people!"[2]

Holy Tuesday

No doubt you feel this way, too, at times, when you face repeated excuses and ultimate rejection of Christ and the Gospel; when you look at a culture without any sacred foundation, a culture that appears to have lost **all** sense; when you deal with people who regard Jesus only as a convenient sidekick, seemingly unaware that those who encountered the living God in the Bible fell on their faces in fear and dread; when you poke into a postmodern life and are told, "If there is any truth, it must be created by me."

At the same time, you continue to seek and meet people who admit that they have no sense of who they are, who do not know how everything fits together, who have no high purpose in life, who wonder why they should go on without any hope. As it has always been, even before St. Augustine said it, their hearts are restless until they find their rest in God.

This week shows clearly that it is through the suffering, death, and resurrection of the Savior that God gathers his people underneath his wings. **This week is for you** standing under the cross as a spiritual beggar. This week is for you whom the Lord fills with good things through the silver chalice of his good news. This week is for you, a witness and a preacher, to give content and validity to your message. This week is for you, showing how everything fits together in the time line of God's history centered at the cross and the resurrection grave.

Letters from a Counselor

This is the week that brought hope to thousands who have gone before you, the week that brings hope to this and the future generations that will follow. This is the week of strong contrasts in the words spoken, from the terrifying "Woe to you, hypocrites!" to the comforting "It is finished!" to the astonishing "He is not here, but he is risen *just as he said*. Go and tell!"

So go and tell, with all your might and joy and conviction! This is why you are where you are at this time in your life's history. This is the time and this is the place to make a difference in people's lives with the only thing that can make a difference in their lives.

God be with you on this Holy Tuesday and throughout this week and the rest of your life! You are a treasured servant in God's world.

In Christ,
Wayne Schulz
Holy Week 2000

Christmas 2000

The Light Shines

"In the beginning was the Word, and the Word was with God, and the Word was God. He was with God in the beginning. Through him all things were made; without him nothing was made that has been made. In him was life, and that life was the light of men. The light shines in the darkness, but the darkness has not understood it" (John 1:1-5).

Breathtaking words! Astonishing! Eye-opening! Spectacular! Foundational!

But for many, mind-boggling.

That last sentence (v. 5) says it all. It's a description of our culture today, a culture that has lost its sacred sense. The light is certainly shining out there, at least if you have anything to do about it. But at times, you think, the world does not see or understand, at least not as rapidly as you wish. You give energy and effort and passion to see to it that the light shines. You enlist, train, and enable the saints to do the same. You plan special times for Christmas worship. You work hard on uplifting sermons and writings and worship and Bible study to let people know that the true Light shines with all the splendor of heaven. You send out and hand deliver hundreds, thousands of invitations to worship the Christ Child.

I am amazed and grateful when daily I think of your efforts. I know that the light shines brightly in your heart. I know that you think your efforts fail because there are still so many people who do not understand the light, who continue to live in darkness, who squander their lives in chaos when the light is so near, so bright, so clear.

But God points you to the bigger picture: **"The light SHINES in the darkness!"(John 1:5).** God keeps working and shining in Christ. That never stops. He uses you in a remarkable way. Think of that!

I see it in the remarks of grateful people who want the church to move forward. I see it in monthly reports, in calls and efforts made. A recent one says: "We're receiving 10 people on Christmas Eve—two adult and two child baptisms (one African-American, two from India)." Amazing! Astonishing!

The Light Shines

The light shines through your efforts! Think of that! Whether you are a missionary or writer or teacher or editor or secretary or an encouraging spouse, let your heart be filled with joy. Concentrate on letting the light shine and making this Christmas a breakthrough time for someone in darkness and spiritual loneliness. You can be confident that some will see, really see the light, and be glad forever. Sometimes you do not see the results until years later. But the light never stops shining.

Luther said that there are three miracles of Christmas: "The first, that God became man; the second, that a virgin was a mother; and the third, that the heart of man should believe this." The LIGHT never stops shining!

Carol writers have often struggled in their attempts to describe these miracles of Christmas. Permit me to share a few stanzas in Old English from Robert Southwell's "New Prince, New Pomp."

> *Behold a simple, tender Babe,*
> *In freezing winter night,*
> *In homely manger trembling lies;*
> *Alas! a piteous sight.*
>
> *Despise Him not for lying there;*
> *First what He is inquire:*
> *An Orient pearl is often found*
> *In depth of dirty mire.*

Letters from a Counselor

The persons in that poor attire
His royal liveries wear;
The Prince Himself is come from heaven:
This pomp is praised there.

With joy approach, O Christian wight!
Do homage to thy King;
And highly praise this humble pomp,
Which He from heaven doth bring.

I truly respect and honor you and your efforts to bring the light of the bright pearl to enlighten the lost for life and to build up the saints for service. If you were not in an exploratory and did not see me so much this year, know that I do not forget you in my prayers. If you and your group need encouragement in reaching out to the lost, let's get a date on the schedule.

Here is a request: after Christmas take some special time with your loved ones and relax in the peace brought by the Light of the world!

In Christ,
Wayne Schulz
Christmas 2000
(Even that is amazing to contemplate!)

Holy Week 2001

Death and Taxes, Bach and BIC

I have two stories for you this Holy Week. They are related (at least in my mind).

One came in the mail last week from our dual-site parish, Peace, in Loves Park and Roscoe, Illinois (I'm on their prospect list!). I received a colorful 5x7 postcard depicting a man weeping in front of a casket on one side and an IRS 1040 on the other, with the calendar date April 15 in the center. The message read, "Only two things are certain, death and taxes." However, "two" was crossed out and "one" was offered as a replacement.

On the back side, in bold print, **"On April 15th find out which one."** It continued, "Sorry, but we really can't do anything about your taxes. Jesus, however, has already done something about death. When he rose from the dead on the first Easter morning, he defeated death—not just for himself, but for all of us! So regardless of your standing with the IRS, join us at Peace Lutheran Church for our Easter celebration on April 15th and hear about the biggest 'refund' of all—Life!"

Only one who knows the meaning of Easter could have written those words.

That is my first story.

The second story occurred last evening. Part of a sacred concert by the Martin Luther College Choir was their rendition of "Jesus, Priceless Treasure," Motet III, by Johann Sebastian Bach. Now, I am convinced that conductors choose that work either to irritate the audience (as my mother said, "It's so long") or to uplift those who have formerly wrestled with it and sung it. I, in the latter category, closed my eyes and enjoyed every word and nuance of sound, remembering each word and note (OK, that's a stretch!) from that initial effort at NWC 40 years ago. Among other things, I remembered singing the words "Lightnings flash and thunders crash" as the lights went out in a terrible thunderstorm in a concert in Wilmot. (So what?! Enough of that!)

Death and Taxes, Bach and BIC

Back at NWC we were basic Midwestern country boys who had merely toyed with basic Bach, maybe a chorale or two. But that September, Prof. Oswald introduced us to the real stuff when he handed out Bach's Motet III. From September to March we wrestled with it, first groaning, then growing to enjoy it (note that I did not say "perfect" it!). In the "doing" of it I sometimes felt like an infant in faith, crying in the night. And here was this giant in faith speaking so powerfully and defiantly. Here was one who could shout at death and thumb his nose at the grave. This is what he said:

DEATH, DEATH, I *do not fear* **thee,**
Though thou standest near me;
GRAVE, GRAVE, I calmly *spurn* **thee,**
Though to dust thou turn me!
Strong in hope and faith.

The truth is the same also in this case.

Only one who knows the meaning of Easter could have written those words and portrayed their meaning so graphically in music.

Bach, even in his death, is still a strong witness and evangelist. That is my second story.

Now, what about BIC? No, I am not suggesting that we add a section to the School of Outreach on "The Performance of Bach for Evangelism," even though I have read that thousands of Japanese have taken an interest in Christianity through listening to Bach cantatas. That may give an idea to some of you.

But in this Holy Week, I think of all those names on your prospect lists, people who may yet be outside of the faith or are mere infants in the faith crying in the night; people who wrestle with questions about life and death, questions about how everything fits together and holds together; people you already know or don't know yet; people you desperately want to reach and enroll in a BIC. It is for them, the lost, that this week took place. It is for them, the lost, that by the light of torches the Light of the world was betrayed by a kiss, rejected by his own, and led away in chains to trial and cross and the resurrection grave.

Romans 8 is the word that God has melted into your heart and the word he cements there once again this week. Romans 8 is the word reflected in the 5x7 postcards sent out in Illinois. Romans 8 is the word that inspired Bach to write Motet III so that choirs would wrestle with and proclaim it even centuries after his death. Romans 8 is the word that God has sent you to bring to the lost, the word that is basic to all meaning and life, the word that is clarified in your Bible Information Classes. And this is the truth that permeates this week and all of life thereafter:

Death and Taxes, Bach and BIC

"Therefore, there is now no condemnation for those who are in Christ Jesus, because through Christ Jesus the law of the Spirit of life set me free from the law of sin and death" (Romans 8:1,2).

Christmas 2001

The Real Lord of the Rings!

Frodo Baggins is an interesting character. Because of the ring he bears, a Ring of Power, the sinister Ringwraiths scurry in hot pursuit of him and the ring. It's a plot of good against evil, a fun read, and perhaps an interesting watch on the silver screen. Yet in the end, it is merely a "so what" story.

Christmas commemorates an event that means everything, the birth of the *real* Lord of the Rings. It stands in adoration of the *Magnum Mysterium*, the great mystery that God takes on human flesh and bones in a place as insignificant as a manger in a sin-scarred and ravished world. It salutes him who is God from God, Light from Light, true God from true God, who brings the supreme sacrifice and gift to the people of his earth.

Letters from a Counselor

Jesus is the real Lord of the Rings, the Bridegroom who looks at us and claims us as his Bride, his Church. He puts his ring of eternal comfort and good hope on us so that we can speak confidently with Paul: "I am convinced that neither death nor life, neither angels nor demons, neither the present nor the future, nor any powers, neither height nor depth, nor anything else in all creation, will be able to separate us from the love of God that is in Christ Jesus our Lord" (Romans 8:38,39). The Lord of the Rings has come. O Bride of Christ, rejoice!

The Lord of the Rings has an awesome place prepared for you. "Come, I will show you the bride, the wife of the Lamb," he says in Revelation 21:9. Take time to read about it in the rest of that chapter! In the meantime, he places you in the apostolic Church. Apostolic ring-bearing people are forward-moving and inviting, as described in the last chapter of Revelation: "The Spirit and the bride say, 'Come!' And let him who hears say, 'Come!' Whoever is thirsty, let him come; and whoever wishes, let him take the free gift of the water of life" (22:17).

Mary lived in the fellowship of the Ring. She knew that the Mighty One had done great things for her. She treasured all these things and pondered them in her heart. She also sang a sturdy hymn of praise that will resound throughout the world again this Christmas.

Joseph portrayed his faith in the Lord of the Rings. Hearing the warning of the angel, he and Mary left in the

The Real Lord of the Rings

middle of the night, physically carrying the child Jesus to safety on a 200+ mile trip to Egypt. One can only wonder in amazement at that effort!

Lisa Beamer was not ashamed to be in the fellowship of the Ring. Her husband was the "Let's roll!" hero of the September 11 flight that crashed in Pennsylvania. Her stirring and confident witness to her faith left her interviewer stunned in silence. Me, too.

Lyle Fredrickson appreciated the fellowship of the Ring. He was a teacher, coach, husband, father, and "Let's roll!" type of chairman in my first congregation. He wanted to see things happen. Recently, he died suddenly when falling from a tree he was pruning.

You, your family, and the group you serve have distinct, treasured, and honored places in the fellowship of the Ring. You amaze me with your preaching, praying, planning, brainstorming, working, and playing as you get to know your community better and then invite its people to come and see what great things God has done for them by sending Christ as Savior and Bridegroom. I thank you for your faithfulness and your efforts to react to the fast changes and challenges of postmodern culture so that the gospel can be proclaimed to the joy and edifying of Christ's holy people, his Bride. Let the joy of Christ be seen in your daily living and caring and in your Christmas messages of eternal hope in Christ!

Letters from a Counselor

Personal greetings to you and your family, Ring-wearers, all of you, in Christ!

Wayne Schulz
Mission Counselor

Holy Week 2002

Clop, Clop, Clop

CLOP, CLOP, CLOP, the sound of a hoofbeat. The figure of a lone man riding on a donkey into Jerusalem. Clop, clop, clop. Deliberate, steady, and resolute. All four of the gospel writers recorded it. With it we began our Holy Week.

So what do we make of this scene? The postmodern man says, "I am not impressed. Other things occupy my attention right now. A king riding a donkey? I prefer relevance."

Relevance is the King riding on a donkey. On Sunday, the 10th of Nisan, each Israelite household selected an unblemished lamb and set it apart for the Lord's sacred purposes. On that particular Sunday, God himself provided a Lamb, the spotless Lamb of God, set apart as sacrifice for the family of the world. Clop, clop, clop. The Lamb of God goes uncomplaining forth to Jerusalem. He must suffer. Must die. Must rise again. What God once told his exiled people finds its ultimate fulfillment. "You will arise and have compassion on Zion, for it is time to show favor to her; the appointed time has come" (Psalm 102:13). Clop, clop, clop. Steady and resolute. The appointed time has come.

"It's Wednesday of Holy Week, and you are reminding me that the appointed time has come?! Me with three sermons to polish, service folders to finish, last-minute invitations to get out to prospects, flurries of questions about Easter breakfast? What I need is an extra day." Think again.

The Scriptures are strangely silent about the events of Holy Wednesday for Jesus. The 13th of Nisan provided a welcome lull before the storm. Wednesday provided quiet hours for Jesus to be in close communion with his heavenly Father.

Right now would be a good time for you to be doing the same. Praying! Pray that God energizes you for this most important weekend. Pray that you proclaim his Word clearly. It's your time to arise and have compassion on Zion. It's your time to show God's favor to his people. It's your appointed time to be at your best in a week in which God gave his best. It's your time to be steady and resolute as you proclaim Jesus to the joy and edifying of

Clop, Clop, Clop

Christ's holy people. It is your purpose to have compassion on Zion and to unleash the power of the cross that energizes life and people for mission to the world. This is not an ordinary week. Your opportunity is not ordinary. Pray! Now!

Sporadic prayer thoughts are running through my mind. Take time now and add to them.

- Thanks to Jesus who is the Light of the world.
- Thanks for the resolute steps of Jesus to Jerusalem.
- Christ has died; Christ is risen; Christ will come again!
- Thanks that Jesus gives us his body and blood and unites us to himself in the Sacrament to forgive, strengthen, and nourish us.
- Thanks for the early Christians who believed in Jesus.
- Thanks for the times of worship and Bible study.
- Thanks that God still uses Word and Sacrament to gather Christians who say, "We believe."
- Thanks for the profound meaning in the words of the Nicene Creed.
- Thanks for the people I met in Alabama on Sunday, searching people, who found our church through a Web site, and now say, "We believe."

Letters from a Counselor

- Thanks for all the people like those above, and they are many. Think of some and pray for them by name. Now!
- Thanks to God who lets us be part of the worshiping and witnessing Apostolic Church.
- Thanks for the times of stress and harsh medicine that refine us and keep us humbly dependent on our Savior.
- Thanks for family and friends who cheer us for this work of bringing God's favor.
- Thanks for family and friends and the many workers and time-givers in the church.
- Thanks that we still love to tell the Story.
- Thanks for all relationships that permit us increasingly to show and to share that Christ has made a difference in our lives. An eternal difference!
- Thanks that we are God's new creations because Jesus rode into Jerusalem on the clop, clop, clop of the donkey.
- Thanks for the hope that we have and the opportunities we can find to extend a message of hope to many who are under the siege of hopelessness.
- Thanks for those who can plan in our midst, for those who see the harvest fields, for those who remind us to get on with the harvest that God gives.
- Thanks for every precious soul who will join us for worship this weekend. Pray that all our

Clop, Clop, Clop

   hearts will go out in joyous welcome to any new faces in our midst.
- Thanks that the following referred to our Savior and not to us who live in his favor: "I looked for sympathy, but there was none, for comforters, but I found none" (Psalm 69:20).

I know that you can pour out your heart to God in behalf of God's people and all those who still may not know who they are and why they exist, that all may find peace and joy in Christ.

A special Holy Week blessing to you and all who surround you with their love and patience!

Wayne Schulz

Christmas 2002

O Light Divine!

**Sent from heaven,
thy rays were given on great and small to shine,
O Light Divine!**

It's been quite a rush since Thanksgiving, including my dad's funeral, a nostalgic trip to preach at my former congregation's 60th anniversary, and everything else in between. This is my first morning to be able to stop, think, reflect, and not to forget that all worship, even at Christmas, is in reality waiting for the Lord. At this hour the words (interspersed here from the song "Heavenly Light") of Alice Mattullath set to music by Alexander Kopylov help me focus on the meaning of Christmas for me, for you, and for all who beg:

Show us the way—unto our God, we pray.

Letters from a Counselor

Life in the parsonage in the WWII days of the 40s vividly taught me the depths of a pastor's life. It made no difference; the great and the small came to my dad's study, some with the loud wailing of shattered lives, some in a search for the whereabouts of a hidden God. Later I saw them leave with quiet resolve, determined to face life once again. "What made the difference?" I often pondered. My father taught me the power and the comfort of the gospel. He also taught me to love people.

**May each soul in sorrow's night
see the heavenly light!**

My heart went out to two veterans of the cross who were sitting in the front pew last week in Rapid City. One was Emma, heading toward her 100th birthday in February, but still as graceful and poised and thankful as she was at 80. The other was Herman, in his 90s, bent over and requiring a cane, but as always a beggar of God's grace and one who respects God's people.

My heart goes out to all the people in your parish area, especially those on your prospect list as friends who need Jesus. I may not know them, but I do pray for them. I think of those searching and those who should be searching more diligently. I think of the unseen sorrows of the first generation of latchkey kids, the despairs of their coming from broken homes, and the absurdities of television sets as surrogate parents. I think of the angry, the broken, the lonely, and the rootless—those who sense

O Light Divine!

the absence of moral absolutes and any substantive reason for hope. *And they are still looking for God.*

> **All those whose feet may falter,**
> **lead unto the sacred altar!**
> **Oh, shine from above, Divine Light of love!**
> **Thou blessing to all creation,**
> **lead us to our salvation!**

If my tired computer does not give up, this message will go out to several hundred of you, all busy, all called by God to be Church—the royal Bride of Christ in the world, all of you beacons of his light to everyone within the sphere of your influence. No matter where or in what capacity you serve or how you relate to people in your witness, I never forget what a force for Christ you are, you royal priests of his, you who show and declare his praises, you who offer and give the Bread of Life freely to all who are seeking something substantial and nourishing. Never tire of being tents for travelers in the wilderness. Never stop singing "Come!" to the weary and burdened. For the Lord is coming to judge the earth. And while we wait and pray and worship and witness, I thank God for you and your loved ones, for all that you do, and for all whom you have led to Jesus.

The Lord be with you. Lift up your hearts!

Letters from a Counselor

Anita joins me in wishing you the special blessings of God, who asks big things of you!

Wayne Schulz
Mission Counselor
Christmas 2002

Holy Week 2003

It's Not What One Would Think

There it is on live television: tanks, armored carriers, Humvees quietly, deliberately, crawling as on cat's paws into Baghdad's central circle. In eerie silence and with rifles poised, cautious marines file out of safe and armored carriers to predetermined positions in the circle. I stare at the scene and wait. And wait. At any moment a noisy, vicious battle will follow, reminiscent of the storming-the-beach scenes in *Saving Private Ryan*. A brave reporter's nervous questions do not distract the soldiers from their scrutinizing focus in every direction and toward every rooftop. Slowly the camera turns to a gum-chewing tank driver who blows a huge bubble and unknowingly breaks the tension. Is this how liberators free a city from an oppressive dictator?!

Letters from a Counselor

It's not what one would think.

With articulate propriety the voice of Lara Logan, CBS reporter, captures the suspense of the moment. But when the statue of Saddam Hussein falls forward in weakness, then smashes to the ground, she abandons political correctness and enthusiastically echoes the pent-up frustrations, jubilation, and relief of those who trample down and beat the fallen statue with their shoes. Weren't the Americans supposed to be the hated ones?

It's not what one would think.

Psalm 68, a processional liturgy, is but one Scripture that describes the activities of God in militaristic terms: "May God arise, may his enemies be scattered; may his foes flee before him.... The chariots of God are tens of thousands and thousands of thousands; the Lord has come from Sinai into his sanctuary" (verses 1,17). From Mount Sinai to Mount Zion to Mount Calvary to the resurrection grave, God is King. The early church believed this psalm foreshadowed the resurrection, ascension, and reign of Christ and the final triumph of his church over the hostile world. But where were the tens of thousands and thousands of thousands of chariots on that Palm Sunday when Jesus marched into Jerusalem? Some might even sneer when they ask you that.

It's not what one would think.

It's Not What One Would Think

By Monday most of the shouting had died down. There were no more "hosannas" to be heard. No doubt many in Jerusalem had forgotten the events of the previous day. After spending a quiet night at nearby Bethany, Jesus returned to Jerusalem. It would be a horrendous week of lies and deceptions and rejections and sufferings and death, a week in which "he came to that which was his own, but his own did not receive him" (John 1:11). Instead of retaliation, however, the Lamb of God would *not* forget the purpose of his coming. People would destroy the temple of his body, but in three days he would raise it again. And the simple truth of all the events of this week and of all of Scripture is that "God was reconciling the world to himself in Christ, not counting men's sins against them" (2 Corinthians 5:19). Now, "if anyone is in Christ, he is a new creation; the old has gone, the new has come!" (2 Corinthians 5:17).

It's not what one would think.

"The Lord announced the word, and great was the company of those who proclaimed it" (Psalm 68:11). Transferred to our times, this is a word for you and me, a word to share, the Word made flesh for our salvation. What a privilege to preach, to teach, to witness, to share this message of life and hope in Christ! "All this is for your benefit, so that **the grace that is reaching more and more people may cause thanksgiving to overflow to the glory of God**" (2 Corinthians 4:15). You may have thought that Easter 2003 would be only one of defeat and bad war news and budgetary shortages and retrenching and being downcast and surviving.

It's not what one would think.

During the last month I have seen evidence of God's grace at work: 20 Hmong baptisms in an extraordinary time of worship, 2 baptisms of unchurched Sunday school children, a family of four confessing their faith in front of a mission congregation, a dedicated servant-leader traveling 66 miles several times a week to keep his congregation going during a year-long pastoral vacancy, some local groups beginning exploratory-like ministries with their own manpower and funds—one of which gathers each Tuesday around the Word and worship and fellowship—this time writing its own Holy Week presentation and play as an outreach tool to the community, a self-supporting congregation adding manpower and working with a vacant mission so that it, too, has pastoral manpower, various missionaries showing schedules filled with Bible information classes, a large number of churches in building projects. Isn't this supposed to be a time of gloom and doom in our synod?!

It's not what one would think.

Among 50 Lenten worshipers at a mission congregation on a quiet April evening, I count 19 young people, one of whom is carrying the book *The Case for Christ* by Lee Strobel. Elsewhere, a young WELS woman

It's Not What One Would Think

works diligently at sharing Christ in the workplace and writes, "As I become more mature in my faith, I find the heritage of our faith very comforting and strengthening—I am proud of it actually." Colleen Carroll in her recent book *The New Faithful—Why Young Adults Are Embracing Christian Orthodoxy* asks, "Why are young adults who have grown up in a society saturated with relativism...touting the truth claims of Christianity with such confidence? Why...are young adults attracted to the trappings of tradition that so many of their parents and professors have rejected? ...Could these young people be proof that the demise of America's Judeo-Christian tradition has been greatly exaggerated?"[3] And reports of vastly overcrowded WELS youth rallies this summer? Take another Easter look at the youth of your congregation and the young people in America!

It's not what one would think.

At times it may seem lonely and difficult in the battles of life and ministry. Where is the needed time? Why don't more people respond? Have I tried to get people to serve and witness through guilt-trip mechanisms? Do I realize how many of them are "exhausted" from their ongoing relational witnessing efforts, as one young person told me? How do I encourage people like that? Have I clearly communicated the joy and peace and freedom the gospel brings? Have I modeled the joy of service to God? How deeply have I failed this time?

Letters from a Counselor

It's not what one would think.

The war has been won. Get its burden off *your* back. That is what the Easter victory is all about! True, fierce skirmishes remain until the day we are called home or the day our Lord returns. But the Lord fights with and for us. With him we march in triumphant procession, we earthen vessels made whole and anew by the blood of Jesus Christ. To him be glory now and forever!

**Praise be to the Lord, to God our Savior,
who daily bears our burdens.
Our God is a God who saves;
from the Sovereign LORD comes escape from death.
(Psalm 68:19,20)**

This is the feast of victory for our God! May you and yours rejoice and be glad in it!

Wayne Schulz
Easter 2003

Christmas 2003

And the Desert Shall Rejoice

"And the desert shall rejoice, and blossom as the rose" (Isaiah 35:1, KJV).

Isaiah wrote from the right side of his brain. How can a desert rejoice?! How can trees clap their hands? No Ents or drab for Isaiah or us when he spoke/sang so poetically about the unfolding of the Scriptures' mighty themes. Before things came to be, he wrote as though they already were. He painted convincing and breathtaking landscapes of the accomplished tasks of God. How uplifting to sit and listen in prayerful contemplation during this holy and meaningful time of the church year! No time, you say? Take time, he says. Too busy? Ponder and keep! You can't? Mary did. Let not the sacred truths of Advent and Christmas bypass your depths and miss those whom you target with a message or witness or greeting or invitation or kindness or smile or gift or hug. "O Light

Divine, shine through this heart of mine." An appropriate pre-Christmas prayer for me. And you!

Back to the *desert* and the *rose* of Isaiah 35:1. You might prefer the "crocus" of the NIV. I predate the NIV and cannot get "rose" out of my mind. In a remembered 1969 concert the choir sang, echoed, and re-echoed this sentence so that it soothed us, passed through us, left the auditorium, and trailed off to eternity: "The desert shall rejoice and blossom as a rose." Reflect on these words in silent admiration. *Hush!* This portrays the divinely intended outcome of the advent and the ministry and the blessing and the completed work of Jesus Christ. *Ponder!* This is the mystery of the Incarnation, the Word made flesh for us cracked clay pots, barren deserts that we are. Into our sand and clay and dryness and desolation and frustration and despair and anguish and hopelessness and lovelessness and carelessness and purposelessness and futurelessness rides the King of kings and Lord of lords.

"Lo, how a ROSE e'er blooming"—in you, in your desert, in your world. He not only blooms, but by his life and death and resurrection he reaches down to you, a sand-crusted beggar at his feet, pulls you out of your tear-stained, dirty little bunker, and says, "Your darkness has disappeared. Your heart shall rejoice, and your joy no one can take from you. In me your life is made whole and wholly held together. I call you my friend. Peace be with you."

And the Desert Shall Rejoice

Now the desert rejoices and blossoms as a rose! In a personal way, this is Isaiah's picture of *you*—the new creation by baptism into Christ, you—the object of God's love and forgiveness, you—the receiver of his Gift, you—the believer of his promises. Ponder that! Deserted no more, your desert rejoices. Shriveled no more, your rose blossoms. Sorrow-filled no more, God wipes away every tear from your despondent eyes. And all the trees of the field clap their hands!

**"O clap your hands, all you people;
shout to God with voice of triumph" (Psalm 47:1, KJV).**

And let the whole earth be filled with his glory!

You, my friends in mission and friends of missions, are more than people on a mission or with a mission. Jesus missionizes you. "I am sending YOU," he says. You prioritize the Great Commission. You promote ongoing relational witnessing. You see and infiltrate the ripe harvest in your sphere of influence. You see the nations now near you. And as God works through your concern and your message, you also need to know that deserts are rejoicing and roses are blossoming in the lives of others. It will not always look that way, but someday you will see and know. Through the good news of the Savior, the whole earth is being filled with God's glory. This occurs when you bring the hope of the message of Jesus to a lost soul. "Lord, let the whole earth *be filled* with your glory!" Pray that. Encourage all in Christ to pray that. And move forward—

In mighty proclamation:
"In Christ is our salvation,"
O night for jubilation!

    Isaiah presents noble thoughts in poetic language. But how is the messy world supposed to understand this? It can't. It can't. The messy world continues in its messiness until you love people enough to bring God's message to bear upon their blind and lost and sinful lives. A missionary writes: "Two of the three people I have the privilege of baptizing next Sunday are teens. One comes from a family where the father killed the mother and then was killed in prison. He lived with his older brother until his brother became so messed up on drugs that he went ballistic. He presently lives with a sister-in-law. The other teen drifts from house to house because his dad left when he was two weeks old and his mom kicked him out at the request of her new boyfriend. The best option he has now is living with a sister whose boyfriend, a gang member, will shortly be getting out of jail. He is already witnessing to both of them and trying to get them to talk with me." It may not look like it, but in those two lives the desert is beginning to rejoice and blossom as a rose.

    "Peace on earth," "A blessed Christmas," and even "Merry Christmas" may not mean much to people still

And the Desert Shall Rejoice

living in a dry and parched desert. Listen to them. Know them. Let your genuine love and concern be demonstrated to them. Let them see the blossoming rose in your life, the beauty of God that reaches out to them with the love of Christ. And help them learn the real meaning of Christmas. For when you speak the Word, God is watering the earth and making it bud and flourish (Isaiah says that, too! Check out chapter 55.)

It may not always appear that way to you. When I see visits made and baptisms and confirmations on report forms, more than anything else I see deserts rejoicing and blossoming. I also see the blossoming rose in the quiet resolve of one who has experienced disappointments in life, yet realizes that it will all finally make sense in heaven. I see it in tears wiped dry at the time of a personal failure or death. I see it in people's eyes and attitudes and smiles and in eager activities for the forward movement of God's Kingdom. I see it in you and your family and your congregation. I see it in your place of learning. I see it in your demeanor at your place of work and your efforts with the people you see daily. I see it in the music you make to magnify the Lord. I see it in your gift for the extension of God's Kingdom. I see it in all the smiling faces of those who know they are loved by God. I thank God that he has made your desert rejoice and blossom—as a rose.

Take a long, deep look at your audience on Christmas Eve. This is a gathering of the saints at the foot of the manger, a reminder that the rose has blossomed in your life and theirs. Take a long look at an individual person God leads into your life so that you can share the good news of Jesus and have the privilege of saying that in Christ "you belong to God." A rose!

Isaiah fully depicts this message in a few verses of his 55th chapter. This is what he says:

**"You will go out in joy and be led forth in peace;
the mountains and the hills will
burst into song before you,**
**and all the trees of the field will clap their hands.
Instead of the thornbush will grow the pine tree,
and instead of briers the myrtle will grow.
This will be for the LORD's renown,
for an everlasting sign, which will not be destroyed"
(verses 12,13).**

Anita joins me in wishing you a Season and a New Year overflowing with blessings in Christ,

Wayne Schulz, mission counselor
Christmas 2003

Holy Week 2004

Do Not Weep!

"Did you cry?" the custodian asked me on the way out of the movie. Perhaps a question she asked everyone every night? I wondered about that. I wondered also whether she had wept, and why it was a concern to her.

> "Do not weep! See, the Lion of the tribe of Judah, the Root of David, has triumphed" (Revelation 5:5).

Well, it didn't look like a victory. Beaten and bludgeoned time after time, slammed and nailed to a rough-hewed cross, he looked like anything but a triumphant conqueror. Maybe you had to turn at times as you watched, and then you noted the reactions of others. Maybe you wondered about them and what they were thinking. Maybe you had to weep in your own anguish at his anguish. Maybe you wept for others—for those who have gone their own way, for those who have not responded to gospel invitations, for those who should have known better, for those who were so defiantly brutal then, and for those who are so callously unmoved now. With a shepherd's heart you wondered about them.

Do not weep.
The Lion of the tribe of Judah has triumphed.

Hopefully that word comforts you. You need to be so comforted in your own heart and faith before you can tell others this Holy Week (and every week) that the Christ of the Passion was not a wimp with no power, no authority, and no purpose. He was, in fact, the Lion of the tribe of Judah, the Messiah who was to come with conquering power (Genesis 49:8-10), yet one who demonstrated that power as the Lamb who was slain. It may not have looked like triumph. And it may not seem to make sense. In fact, it seems foolish.

"For the foolishness of God is wiser than man's wisdom, and the weakness of God is stronger than man's strength" (1 Corinthians 1:25).

The atoning sacrifice of Christ's death is the key to all the counsels of God. This is the heart of everything, the power that opens the Bible, the balm that removes tears and opens hearts to joy and wisdom and strength and salvation! There is hope in One alone, in the slain and triumphant Messiah!

Do Not Weep!

"Greater love has no one than this,
that he lay down his life for his friends"
(John 15:13).

He can take the book and reveal and execute the counsels of God. His appearance evokes a new chorus of adoration from the living creatures and elders, from thousands of angels, and from every creature in God's world:

"You are worthy to take the scroll and to open its seals,
because you were slain,
and with your blood you purchased men for God
from every tribe and language and people and nation.
You have made them to be a kingdom and priests
to serve our God,
and they will reign on the earth (5:10)" (Revelation 5:9,10).

How awesome to be made worthy by Christ to be part of this, kings and priests in God's kingdom, to be able to love and to speak with the transforming power of the good news! How great to be able to find ways to love the neighbor, to bless the community and its people—more and more from every tribe and language and nation, to thank God that here and now there is the pleasure to live in his kingdom and to serve him—without grumbling or complaint!

Letters from a Counselor

Because Christ served you beyond measure, it is your privilege to serve in selfless love, to be orthodox in your beliefs *and* genuinely caring in your life. It is your business to get on with life as one who really "gets" it, who understands what the status of holiness means and requires, who exudes demonstration of Christ's love along with generous doses of proclamation of Christ's love. You can live with purpose because Christ has given you a purpose. You can smile as though you know something special because you do know something special. You can move from your computer and your room, meet people, listen to people, care for people, and feed people who are starving for hope because you know that only Jesus provides food that does not perish and brings hope that will not fade away.

The Lion of the tribe of Judah has triumphed. That immeasurable truth is spread out extra-generously for you this Holy Week. Will you weep as the scenes pass in front of you and grip your heart? Tears of remorse and repentance are important. Even more important is that with renewal from Word and Sacrament your tears will cease and you will believe, live, and proclaim with fresh energy and positive tone the triumph of the Lion of the tribe of Judah.

May God bless you and yours this week!
Wayne Schulz
Mission Counselor

CHRISTMAS 2004

GOD IS WITH US

Rejoice and be exceeding glad!

The Word became flesh and made his dwelling among us" (John 1:14). Don't speed over those words this Christmas. Slow down when you read them, when you hear them. Pause. Stop. Let the message speak, hit home, penetrate hearts, your heart. This is not a haphazard Christmas gift. It is from God. *Is* God. God's one and only Son. God's excellence in full humanity. For you! *O magnum mysterium!*

There is nothing shoddy or mediocre about Immanuel, this Gift of "God with us." Mary knew it: "...the Mighty One has done *great things* for me—*holy* is his name" (Luke 1:49). And she knew the Gift's greater impact: "His *mercy extends* to those who fear him, from generation to generation" (Luke 1:50). In his birth, in his life, in his death, in his resurrection, in his promise to come again, and in his judgment, Christ is with us. Be comforted. Comfort! Speak tenderly to Jerusalem. Lift up your voice and say to your communities, "Here is your God!"

Personal fear and uncertainty about your status with God? God is with you. Unsure about the future and your part in it? God is with you. Not sure you are using your gifts to full advantage? God is with you. Sensed lack of support from coworkers and leaders, from members and acquaintances, from those you have bent over to help, even from those close to you? God is with you—in forgiveness, in presence, in direction, in certainty, into eternity. God is with you in Christ, in the Word made flesh, in the Gift of Bethlehem, in the Light of the world, in excellence. What can be better than the excellence of this Gift?

Because God's excellence in Christ came to us in insignificant Bethlehem, greater things were yet to come. The Word lived with us. The Word died for us. The Word kept his promise and rose again. The Word is in us and gives us a word of solace for this and every age: "I am with you always, to the very end of the age" (Matthew 28:20).

> Dear Christian friend, on him depend;
> Be of good cheer and let no sorrow move you.
> For God's own child in mercy mild
> *Joins you to him—how greatly God must love you!*
> (*Christian Worship: A Lutheran Hymnal* [CW] 40:3).

God Is With Us

On December 12, I stood in admiration of these thoughts when I observed Moira Grace's (grandchild #5) baptism into God's excellence in Christ. This occurred in the setting of a Canadian gymnasium, familiar to many of you in start-up churches, not in architectural splendor and majesty, but in all the excellence of the sacramental presence of God with us. God can be present and do remarkable things in small and inconspicuous places—just like Bethlehem.

One hour northwest of Toronto lies Elora, Ontario, a small and inconspicuous village—just like Bethlehem. Our trip there in the late afternoon of December 12 reminded us of a nostalgic painting and photogenic Christmas setting—huge and thick snowflakes falling gently, quaint village homes and shops decked out for Christmas, a lighted brick church with a tall steeple welcoming well-dressed folks walking to a concert in the fresh-falling snow. The Elora Festival Singers were poised to present Handel's *Messiah* in the crowded church.

I have often listened to Handel's *Messiah* on records and CDs. But what would a live performance of it be like here in this wintry setting in Elora, Ontario? Would it be worth the slippery trip to sit next to people we did not as yet know? Would it be a mediocre effort? In anticipation we sat and waited and wondered. Concentration increased as the singers began and responded to every slight move of the conductor's hands and eyes, singing the awesome words into our hearts, making us think as we listened. Old and middle-aged people stared straight ahead. Young people leaned forward and bowed their heads in the intensity of the words, "For as in Adam all die, so in Christ all will be made alive" (1 Corinthians 15: 22). The message and the conducting and the singing and the phrasing and the quality and the attention to details were evident to everyone. Back into the winter wonderland, we wondered how such excellence could come out of a small place and how we could have been so blessed to be there.

As in Bethlehem, there was no mediocrity in Elora.

So how are we doing this week? Tired? In a frenzy with the schedule? Can't wait until it's all over? Whether or not we are full-time *proclaimers* of God's Word, all of us are *demonstrators* of that Word made flesh for us. Does not the excellence of God at Bethlehem drive us to let his light shine through us, to do our best in our morning greetings to other busy people, to work on our caring attitude and love to the neighbor, to encourage brothers and sisters with the good news that emanated from Bethlehem and pierced the sky with God's special light?

I pray that many will come to what you think is your inconspicuous place, wondering what they will see and hear. I pray that you will give everyone God's excellence and not your mediocrity. The time is right, and

God Is With Us

it is here now, to magnify the Lord who has done great and excellent things for you. And holy is his name.

Anita joins me in thanking you for all you have done and will do to reach people with the good news that came from Bethlehem. I feel that I have been blessed by your efforts. Blessings for Christmas and the New Year!

Wayne Schulz
2004

Holy Week 2005

The Lord Needs a Donkey

While pounding the pavement in recent weeks, I marveled at how much is carted along in the car's trunk. Anything remotely needed for each trip must be in there, and I must carry it with me. With my filled trunk, I keep thinking about that lowly pack animal donkey that clop-clopped Jesus into Jerusalem when his hour had come. Much has been written about this donkey. It is amazing that Jesus knew where to find it and what its owner would say and do when told, "The Lord needs it." Imagine that. The Lord needs—a donkey.

The Lord needs a donkey.

You know the deep meaning of this week. You rejoice in the culmination of Jesus' ministry. You believe in what Jesus did for all in perfect fulfillment of prophecy, in completing the will of the heavenly Father. This Passion Week establishes the heart of your faith and leads to the joy of Jesus' resurrection, the beating heart of humanity's hope. It all started with the clopping donkey carrying the Lamb of God, the Lion of the tribe of Judah, into Jerusalem. Rejoice in the Savior and all he accomplished that week! Admire the privileged donkey for which the Lord had need.

> **"You, Lord, are both Lamb and Shepherd.**
> **You, Lord, are both prince and slave"**
> (Sylvia Dunstan, "Christus Paradox").

Have you ever thought about yourself as a "donkey" for whom the Lord has need? It may be worth the contemplation.

The Lord packs you up and loads you with his good *gifts.* "He has filled the hungry with good things" (Luke 1:53). "He has raised up a horn of salvation for us" (Luke 1:69). He anoints our heads with oil; our cups overflow (Psalm 23). "He has rescued us from the dominion of darkness and brought us into the kingdom of the Son he loves, in whom we have redemption, the forgiveness of sins" (Colossians 1:13,14). No wonder the hymn writer Kurt J. Eggert could describe God's grace in Christ as being "so rich, so wide, so high, so free" (CW 392:4). As you clop through daily life, you carry this rich cargo of gifts and your one-of-a-kind giftedness with you.

The Lord Needs A Donkey

"Follow me," Jesus says as he leads you through a life of service. Clop, clop, clop you go, day after day. This is not always easy to do. No one ever said it would be easy to be a servant taking up the cross in the servant-hood of Jesus. You understand what that means in this busy week. You understand what that means when some reject the gift of Jesus or claim it's only good for you. Yet Jesus invites, "Come to me…and I will give you rest" (Matthew 11:28). To your burdened back come his massaging words that dismantle stubborn mule-headedness: "My yoke is easy and my burden is light" (Matthew 11: 30). Refreshed, you can walk again with head held high, with ears perked, with ever-hastening and directed clop-clops.

The donkey carried Jesus into the city of death and resurrection. In ways that are similar yet dissimilar, you also are a *Jesus-carrier* into your area of influence. Fathom with meekness the remarkable words of St. Paul: "I have been crucified with Christ and I no longer live, but Christ lives in me" (Galatians 2:20). You wear Christ through baptism. In you Christ lives by faith. In your new life you represent Christ. You are a letter of recommendation for him when you clop, clop, clop through life this week, this year. Life is never mundane and dreary and without purpose for Jesus-carriers.

Every day and everywhere you go, you carry Jesus with you—his love, his forgiveness, his light, his salt, his water of life, his bread of life. To the poor and needy and burdened and hurting and searching and disheartened you clop. To those crying to be heard, you listen with the ears of Jesus. To those wounded by sin and death, you hold out the soothing balm of Jesus' healing prescription. Jesus needs you to take his good news and eternal life to all creation. Jesus needs you, you clopper of his in the world of people he loves, you who walk in his ways with praise and thanksgiving on your lips, you with Jesus at your side, his Word in your heart and on your lips, his love that desires to reach your neighbors and your relationships.

Jesus promises to be with his cloppers to the very end of the age. He is for you, in you, with you, in front of you, behind and beside you every clop along the way. His Word is a lamp to your feet and a light for your path—there is no reason to wander aimlessly.

"Darkness is daylight when Jesus is there" (CW 367:1).

Remember that truth in the celebration of the Lord's Supper and in the darkness of Good Friday. Discover joy and delight in the splendor and daylight of the resurrection. Move forward with sure-footed and beautiful feet as you clop, clop, clop to others with Jesus at your side, as you go to the people for whom he died and rose. The Lord has need of you to move him through the mud of people's lives so that they see in him the life that washes them and changes them for all eternity.

Christ-proclaimers, Christ-demonstrators, Christ-shiners, Christ-carriers, Christ-connectors, Christ-

The Lord Needs A Donkey

introducers, Christ-lovers, and Christ-livers—this describes all of you in one way or another. It is my privilege to know you, work with you, and address you this Holy Week. May Jesus' love and victory give direction and purpose and joy to every step you take, to every person you meet, to every neighbor you love.

> In Christ,
> Wayne Schulz
> March 22, 2005

Christmas 2005

Christus Paradox in the Manger

What do Alex Adamopoulos, Rich Gross, Tracey Ross, Al Cisneros, Daren Grant, Mary Salinas, Greg Cameron, and Sandy Potter have in common? Each drives an Infiniti G35. Alex, for instance, is featured in a half-page ad in the *Wall Street Journal*. The ad says little about the Infiniti except that it has "intelligent all-wheel drive." The ad, however, says much about Alex's successful life and his relationship with his Infiniti. The point is, you, too, can have a relationship with an Infiniti and your name can be listed on the Web site. In today's culture, the connection to the product is the main thing, a story to be celebrated and imitated and told.

It's Advent. A voice from the past booms, "Prepare the way of the Lord!" Preparation points to your needed connection with the manger, your relationship with the Babe in the manger. It may be tempting to move past the manger as quickly as possible, to trivialize the manger's meaning, to regard it as a distraction, or to prefer an ordinary schedule and a real ministry once again.

Go back to the manger. Take another look. God was up to something big there. He did not give us sentimentality. He gave us a person, his Son, the Babe lying in the manger. Reflect on your connection with the manger. Does it give you a story to believe and celebrate and tell?

Go to the manger! What do you see there? *Christus Paradox* is lying there—

> **The everlasting instant—**
> **Lamb and Shepherd, prince and slave,**
> **peacemaker and swordbringer, scorned and craved,**
> **clothed in light and stripped of might,**
> **shining in eternal glory, beggar'd by a soldier's toss,**
> **one both gift and cost,**
> **who walks beside us and sits in power at God's side,**
> **proclaims a way that's narrow,**
> **has a love that reaches wide,**
> **Worthy is our earthly Jesus! Worthy is our cosmic Christ!**
> **Worthy his defeat and vict'ry.**
> **Worthy still his peace and strife.**
> **You in manger are both death and life.**
> **Alleluia!**
> (Word-picture phrases from Sylvia Dunstan's "Christus Paradox" sung recently at Wisconsin Lutheran Seminary)

Christus Paradox in the Manger

O Mighty Mystery! A sermon there in every line, a witness handle in every word! Go to the manger and kneel before the Way, the Truth, and the Life—God's love for all humanity. Go to the manger and focus on the mystery of God's presence and love and purpose—the Babe who came to seek and save the lost. Go to the manger. Sit there awhile. Contemplate. It is God in there, God in the relationship business with his created people, God in his unique way of reaching down to us. The manger scene is his ad, his invitation, his come strategy, "Come to me, and I will give you rest." Rest and linger there at the manger scene. Lying there is Jesus, the Lord's Christ—

who is,
who was,
who is to come,

like none other, the only thing that counts in your life in the final analysis.

There in the manger is God's connection with the hurricanes of distressed lives, his sign that he keeps his Word, that he loves and longs for people devastated by war and terrorism and unfaithfulness and relativism. There in the manger is God's rest and relief for all who are wearied and burdened in their false and futile pursuit of foundation and meaning and security. There in the manger God unveils shallowness in the postmodern onslaught of inerrant political correctness. There is God's forgiveness, his right for all the world's wrongs. There is hope for the hopeless. Help for the helpless. There is a life-giving connection for disconnected lives. There is the one relationship that makes a difference in your life, the one who desires you to network with others and to make a difference in their lives. There is the great and mighty wonder of God's Incarnation, a scene to take to heart and cherish and celebrate. Immanuel—God is with us. O that all the world would stop and stare and sing, every voice in concert ring,

"Alleluia!"

As Paul did, take the manger's occupant with you this season, this New Year. "I have been crucified with Christ and I no longer live, but Christ lives in me. The life I live in the body, I live by faith in the Son of God, who loved me and gave himself for me" (Galatians 2:20). Take him, both scorned and craved, with you. Take him to the hungry, the hurt, the thirsty, the desperate, the despondent. For there is renewal and fullness of life in the Christ Child of the manger. There is an eternal future in him "who was and who is and who is to come."

Your Infiniti G35 (or whatever your preferred model of transportation may be) does not make or define you. The Christ of the manger and the cross and the resurrection grave makes and remakes you, always in his image, always growing in him, always working and loving and sharing and proclaiming in the fullness of your life which he provides. Into your part of the world he places

Christus Paradox in the Manger

you and stands beside you as you live and go and work and love and witness while it is day.

Anita joins me in thanking you for your service and efforts, your faithfulness, and your going forward in Jesus' name. Contemplate the manger. Celebrate Christmas with Jesus and your loved ones. Rejoice in the Lord—always; and again I say, REJOICE!

Wayne Schulz
2005

HOLY WEEK 2006

OH, AND JESUS DIDN'T DIE ON THE CROSS?

Have you noticed the emerging onslaught throughout Lent and Palm Sunday this year? The mainstream media are filled with it. It's in your face at Borders and other major book suppliers. The blogs are reacting, some bad, some good, some remarkable in insights, some finding a voice where people really listen and speak eloquently.

First, there is the feverish prelude to the release of the movie *The Da Vinci Code* in an effort to question or nullify Christian understanding. To foment doubt? Possibly? Second, the Judas documents sneak in so innocently. Let's see, Judas the favored disciple in a plot with Jesus? He whom Jesus called "a devil" (John 6:70)? Poor Judas—don't be so prejudiced about him? Third, consider the PBS Palm Sunday program "The Great Fire of

Rome." There we learned that the fire which destroyed Rome was not set by kind and considerate Nero (kind enough to burn Christians alive), but, get this, by mean-spirited and boisterous Christians acting out prophecies in the book of the Revelation to St. John. Finally, in case you have not heard enough, there is the latest "theory" which someone came up with about Good Friday and which NBC's *Dateline* thought good to "explore" because of its "interest to the large Christian community." **Oh, so Jesus didn't really die on the cross??**

Ancient heresies in new wrappings. Could there be an agenda here, an anti-Christian way of noting the Easter season—to destabilize the Christian community? As someone said last Friday, "All these *don't* serve that (Christian) community, *but another.*" Right on!

On a recent Web log about the Judas story, a blogger wrote: "It is funny that the same people who are so eager to impugn the truth of the four canonical Gospels are suddenly devotees of the literal truth and integrity of this one (the Judas one), which was rejected by the early Christian church as a canonical source. An interesting historical source? By all means. A refutation of the Christian faith? Risible."

Take to heart what Jesus said: "Blessed are you when people insult you, persecute you and falsely say all kinds of evil against you *because of me. Rejoice and be glad,* because great is your reward in heaven, for in the same

Oh, and Jesus Didn't Die on the Cross?

way they persecuted the prophets who were before you" (Matthew 5:11,12).

But Holy Week is not about us and our sense of persecution. It's about Jesus and the completion of his agenda for the world, for us. In Philippians 2, the same chapter in which we are encouraged to humility—"Your attitude should be the same as that of Christ Jesus" (verse 5)—we are also invited to "shine like stars in the universe as you hold out the word of life" in a "crooked and depraved generation" (verse 15).

You who proclaim publicly from the pulpit, it is essential this year to shine like the stars as you preach with power the Christ who was crucified and who has risen for the sins of the world. You who serve and love and witness and invite and share at work and at home or school, shine like the stars and with great love and understanding toward those who are wounded by this world's fevered onslaughts against Christ and his followers. This is the week that changed everything for you, for the world. Let Jesus speak. Let his truth remove the fog, the smog, the foul stench that wishes to linger and lurk and hide where people learn and hang out.

Instead of lies and doubt, let there be TRUTH running over in rich measure. Instead of sin, let there be forgiveness. Instead of weakness of faith, let there be the gospel in Word and sacraments to build a powerful faith and strong life that walks as a disciple of Jesus. Instead of hopelessness and depression, let there be the hope that we have in Jesus. Instead of death, let there be life, life that comes from him who rose, who is alive, who walks among us, who dwells within us, who calls us to himself and lifts up our eyes from this place of darkness. Instead of fear, let there be boldness to serve and love and share the truth that upholds and sustains and compels us to move forward and to meet culture head-on with the Jesus of Holy Week and resurrection morn.

This is a week of palms and whips, jubilation and jeers, death and life. So much more than chocolates and eggs and bunnies! The liturgies of this week are powerful and primal. For nearly two thousand years God's people have gathered with palms and candles and prayers and silent meditation and bread and wine and proclamation of the fullness of the good news of Jesus. All because he did die on the cross; he did rise from the dead. Here is reason and motivation to shine like the stars of the universe as you hold out the Word of Life.

Oh, and Jesus Didn't Die on the Cross?

This Holy Week our journey takes us to Washington to proclaim Jesus to people I don't know as yet and to be with our children who next week are expecting the birth of a baby with spina bifida and surgery after birth. It is a new journey for us and them, one that could cause fear and consternation had Jesus not lived and died for us, had he not risen from death. Please pray for this baby even as you join me in thanksgiving for the gift of baptism that unites us to the Jesus of Holy Week.

May the blessings of Jesus lift you up and make you strong in life!

Wayne Schulz
Mission Counselor
Holy Week 2006

Christmas 2006

Grinch

Some Grinch stole the "holiday" trees at SeaTac—blah, blah, blah—for days. After swift and loud reactions, workers marched them back on carts. Now, 80 mph winds pound rain-drenched SeaTac. Tall evergreens, symbols of Christmas, flattened. SeaTac tree talk, no electricity, all too much the week before Christmas.

A Christmas tree in church was not regarded as a noble practice in early American Lutheranism. Here, in part, is how one early Missouri Synod congregation reacted to a church tree scene, as quoted in the Cranach blog:

> It was Christmas Eve, 1851. Rev. Henry Schwan stood at the door of the Zion Church of Cleveland, Ohio, welcoming the hundred or so members of his new congregation. When at last he closed the door, he walked slowly up the

aisle toward a beautiful, green tree glistening in the light of candles - the first Christmas tree at an American Christmas service. There had been other trees in a few scattered homes, but none before had ever been placed in a church. The congregation stared. After Rev. Schwan read the Gospel story of the Nativity, he felt closer to his people this Christmas than ever before. But those feelings boomeranged.

"What business did a foreigner have decorating a tree in honor of Christ?" demanded one man, not a member of Schwan's congregation. "'Twas idolization, pure idolization!" another non-parishioner muttered. "Blasphemous!" said a third. "We won't let it happen again next year!"

Finally, the outsiders talked of bringing Rev. Schwan's action to the attention of the sheriff, the mayor, the governor. But the townspeople were reminded that the Constitution of the United States guaranteed freedom of worship, even for the new immigrants, even to taking vulgar, candlelit trees into church at Christmas. Even so, one way remained to stop such practices - there was no law forcing Christians to do business with pagans.[4]

Grinch

What about the baby Jesus?

This year I saw Scrooge in *A Christmas Carol* in downtown Madison, a place where Christ's name is supposed to be suppressed. Jesus is not in the play. Yet there is a hint of him in the preface where Dickens says he wanted to write "a whimsical kind of masque" that might "awaken some loving and forbearing thoughts, never out of season in a Christian land," especially when Tiny Tim "hoped the people saw him in the church, because he was a cripple, and it might be pleasant to them to remember upon Christmas Day, who made lame beggars walk, and blind men see." A somewhat cryptic portrayal of the baby Jesus? Kudos, however, to the carolers in the play strolling not with "Jingle Bells" but with stalwart carols that depict Jesus as Savior.

What about the baby Jesus?

The rhetoric is fierce. "They are trying to take Christmas away from us." Here are notes that appeared in *First Things*:

> The struggle to keep Christ in Christmas never ends. The Episcopal Cathedral of St. John the Divine...is doing its part. They have a twenty-eight-foot-tall metal spiral sculpture that is a "Tree of Sounds" as part of the Winter Solstice Celebration. "This popular secular event," it says here, "celebrates the ancient

traditions from which Christmas has evolved." Any other questions about the true meaning of Christmas?

 Religious leaders seem to be at a loss about the significance of Christmas once commercialism has been removed. But this is not the worst of it. After an excess of outrage against the hazards of commercialism, this statement by church leaders offers no other Gospel to those it has condemned than phrases like these: "the spirit of Christmas," "making Christmas real," "invest in renewing our own spirits, our relationships, and our natural environment," and "the spiritual and life-affirming potential of the season." Great balls of fire! The most you can affirm is the same meaningless jargon that is readily used by the very merchants, advertisers, and media you condemn.... Christmas is about the birth of Jesus of Nazareth, the incarnation of the second Person of the Holy Trinity. Of this there is not one word...in the statement of the Campaign to Take Commercialism Out of Christmas. Believing that when people are truly serious they can afford to lighten up, Pastor Klein told the NCC that he was going to preach on advent during Advent. "And then a little later in the season I'll pour some brandy in the eggnog and give my daughter that REM tape she's been

GRINCH

wanting and have a merry Christmas—in honor not of my moral sensitivity but of the birth of Mary's boy."[5]

Jesus was missing already in 1993.

Now it is Christmastime 2006. Where is the baby Jesus in your life? Where is the baby Jesus in the lives of so many spiritually hapless, homeless, helpless? Where is Jesus in the lives of our neighbors, coworkers, friends, schoolmates? My grandson Evan has been in trouble at school both for telling kids there is no Santa and talking about "church stuff." He was told that you should not talk about religion in front of other people because it makes them uncomfortable. And he lives in the Bible Belt. The same goes for grandchildren in Canada: "The boys are getting hammered with persecution. Jonah, who regularly has been defending the faith and witnessing to Christ to all who will listen, is regularly made fun of by the people in his class to the point that he is very afraid to talk about Jesus and the real reason for Christmas right now...of course we are encouraging him forward in the Word, but our boys are really out there on the battlefield taking some hits right now." In the *Harvard Crimson*, the psychologist Steven Pinker argued that the persistence of religion is "an American anachronism...in an era in which the rest of the West is moving beyond it." Does all this "moving beyond Jesus" sound familiar to you? Too familiar?

Look at other trees and see Jesus.

Letters from a Counselor

"After he drove the man out, he placed on the east side of the Garden of Eden cherubim and a flaming sword flashing back and forth to guard the way to the tree of life" (Genesis 3:24). Even though people try as they may to find ways for internal peace and direction for life, God does not want them to look for that in Eden. Man-made attempts to find and restore Eden in their lives are fruitless. They end with disillusionment and ultimate despair. God pointed to another tree, *the tree of the cross* on which the Savior of the world would hang with the sins of all of us. Life, fullness of life, comes from the Savior on that tree. Finally, and we all wait, there is the *tree of life in Paradise*. "Blessed are those who wash their robes, that they may have the right to the tree of life and may go through the gates into the city" (Revelation 22:14).

Trees, not necessarily Christmas trees, have center place in God's plan for us.

So here we stand once more at another Christmas, sometimes dismayed by the letters to the editor and the open opposition to anything that represents Jesus. Sometimes overwhelmed by the amount of required preparatory work. Sometimes fearing that "peace on earth" will never come to many who are so bent on terror instead. Sometimes wondering whether we will partner with each other seriously to bring Jesus to those who are still searching for the way to the tree of life.

At times like this simple words stand out: "Born of the virgin Mary...suffered...died...rose again." Simple

GRINCH

words that ground us. Powerful words that point to Christ and spell freedom for us sin-slaved, guilt-burdened, and death-destined people. Words that revive us, stand us on our feet again to live new lives in Jesus, with Jesus, and for Jesus. Words that those around us, near and far, need to hear.

Our mission in life is to say something about this Jesus, the Word made flesh. As imitators of God, living a life of service in Jesus, bridges will be built to the hearts of others. As proclaimers of Christ, hearts will be stirred, convicted, and made alive. In these last days, God speaks to us and the world through his Son. As the Christ Child strides out from the pages of the Scriptures directly into daily lives, there are and will be collisions, negative and positive. Yet the forward march must continue, for Jesus is the Word and the Truth and the Life humanity must see and hear.

We know the language of the tragedy of life. We also know the joy of new life in Christ. *"Joy to the world, the Lord has come!"* Repeat, repeat that sounding joy! Again and again! No matter what the Grinches say. Know that your life, your witness, and your efforts are appreciated. Gather around the tree of life with your flock. Sing those stalwart carols. March into 2007 even more determined that God is using you to make a difference among those who still seek life in Eden, wherever that is, or amid the trees in this world's bleak wilderness.

Letters from a Counselor

Anita joins me in greeting you, thanking you, and asking God's blessings for you along the way of life with Jesus right next to you.

Wayne Schulz
Christmas 2006

Holy Week 2007

Attitude

It is the beginning of Holy Week. Fatigue paws its way in. Busyness, weariness from thinking, writing, preaching, teaching, caring, inviting. Looking forward to next week? Hearing others talk about spring break trips—but none for you? Time for an attitudinal checkup.

"Your attitude should be the same as that of Christ Jesus" (Philippians 2:5).

It's a sentence we read or heard on Palm Sunday. It's a sentence that moves directly to the beauty of Jesus and his self-giving humility and sacrifice. This attitude, this humility is yours because Jesus has made you his own, has incorporated you into himself by baptism. Imagine what life would be like without that first Holy Week. "Had Christ who once was slain, not burst his three-day prison," (CW 160) what then? Then the real reason for weariness would triumph. But that is not the case. Not the case. This week is the startling reminder that Jesus "was delivered over to death for our sins and raised to life for our justification" (Romans 4:25). This is more than a PowerPoint presentation on a big screen: **Jesus, true God from true God, became sin for us.**

Really? Can you say that again? Not everyone gets it, but everyone has been invited to hear about it. That is why you are important to God's mission on earth. You are his Light-reflector, his Truth-proclaimer. You are an example, an icon through which people will see Jesus, a witness to point to Jesus.

All of this creates a *new attitude of humility* for us, a new way of looking at everything that stands in the way of true unity. "Your attitude should be the same as that of Christ Jesus." Wow! Me, a Christ-like attitude-carrier? Yes! I can no longer dance lightly over the impact of that verse to get at the meat of the verses that follow. Together with discipleship comes Christian responsibility which Christ himself inspires and gives.

> "Lord, by the stripes which wounded you,
> From death's sting free your servants, too,
> That we may live and sing to you.
> Alleluia!" (CW 148:5).

ATTITUDE

Our faith grows and glows from the images and messages of this week. Our attitude, our speech, and our way of life show that we are in the camp of Jesus as his Light-reflectors. We know that he came to make us his special people, to shine in and through us to others. We dare not hoard his glory for ourselves. We will not focus only on ourselves. The fruit of Christ's victory makes us his celebrities whose hope is in God, not in idols. We are not like American celebrities who crave attention for themselves. As God's celebrities we are new creations with Jesus-attitudes, displayed in loving concern and lives of service.

This Holy Week seems like a new beginning for me, the first time since Christmas that I have communicated with some of you. For me everything changed abruptly on January 4. Having never been a hospital patient, I soon became familiar with the Scan family (Cat, Pet, Bone). I heard a doctor tell me kindly, "I am 98% sure that this is lung cancer, but we will have to do a bronchoscope to find out what type and to determine treatment." Dozens of times I faced the question, "So, did you smoke?" Well, "No, I don't fit the pattern." The treatment was a major surgery called a pneumonectomy.

I remember my son Jason being asked to write the initials of the surgeon on the left side of my chest so that the correct lung would be removed. I remember being wheeled to the pre-op room as on a crowded freeway since there were 55 surgeries there that day. I remember a child crying sadly in a nearby pre-op room and praying for that child. I remember praying for others on my list. I remember stating my name and birth date to everyone I saw in that room. I remember visually the kindness of the surgery attendants. And I remember "coming to" in that same pre-op area and feeling overjoyed that it felt natural to breathe. I was in that post-surgery area for over five hours because they had nowhere else to take me.

Most of all, I remember people, so many people who had **"the attitude the same as that of Christ Jesus."** There was my surgeon who prepares for surgery by going into the chapel to pray. There were supportive nurses who shared their life stories, some of whom told me sincerely that they were praying for me. There were catheter collectors, usually young helpers who appeared so dutifully every morning at 4:30. There were WELS pastors and other friends who stopped in with God's Word. There was my roommate who was very moved by the encouraging words the pastors and others brought since his pastor would not think of coming; my roommate who was not WELS but had a subscription to *Meditations;* my roommate whose wife could not pick him up from the hospital because she had a game of Bridge to attend to—I was ready to get up and haul him home. I remember the Gen-X young woman who brought up my food one night, saw me reading *Meditations,* and said, "Oh, I read that, too." All this in Madison which is so politically correct that one is led to believe it is illegal to talk about God!

Attitude

I remember a supportive wife and family, an unbelievable number of greetings, cards, and reports of prayers being said. Phone calls from unexpected sources. This is almost overwhelming to me. But not quite. Because all around us examples of caring attitudes abound, attitudes like that of Christ Jesus.

I thank God for all of this and all of you. I humbly give thanks that Holy Week's events and meaning are deeply embedded in so many people, people I regard as God's unheralded celebrities who march through life with his Truth and Light as part of their being, people who understand why they have and use their Christ-like attitudes.

May God bring blessings to your caring and proclaiming this Holy Week.

In Christ,
Wayne Schulz
Holy Week 2007

Christmas 2007

Christ to the World with Joy We Bring

"The people that walked in darkness
have seen a great light.
They that dwell in the shadow of death,
upon them hath the light shined" (Isaiah 9:2, KJV)

A pastoral conference once debated a question, "What kind of guys were the shepherds? Feared and hated? Or soft and gentle, as some artists depict them?" It is an interesting discussion. What matters, however, is that in their shadow of death and to their darkness a great light came. What matters is that in their presence an angel of the Lord appeared, and the glory of the Lord shown around them. What matters is that a great company of the heavenly host appeared with the angel and praised God. What really matters is what the shepherds in their spiritual and physical darkness heard:

Hodie Christus natus est! **Today Christ is born!**

Letters from a Counselor

That is God's exclamation mark on his Old Testament promises, an exclamation of relief and peace for his people. News of great joy for all to hear. Let the angels sing about it. Let the shepherds hurry and proclaim it to all who will listen. Let hearts be glad and sing for joy. Proclaim to the ends of the earth—the message, the person, the truth that

God is with us.

Where have angels been singing lately? On first thought, I have not heard much from the heavenly choirs in recent days/years. There are 20-some days before the Iowa caucuses. Who will be the anointed one in either party? In the long lineup of primaries, will it really make a monumental difference to the nation or to the world? Will the angelic choirs sing about the glory of God at the culmination of those caucuses? Are heavenly choirs singing loudly at NFL playoff games? At bowl games where thousands gather and could hear? On the magnificent skating rink in New York City? In our churches as visible guest choirs? Where are the angels rejoicing today? How about in your heart, in your songs of praise, and through your shepherd-like self and actions in whatever calling your Lord has taken you in your life?

**"Once again my heart rejoices
As I hear far and near sweetest angel voices.
'Christ is born!' their choirs are singing
Till the air *everywhere* now with joy is ringing"(CW 37:1).**

CHRIST TO THE WORLD WITH JOY WE BRING

It still matters today that Christ was born, that in him God is with you and the world, that you join with others in singing about it. It still matters that sin-covered people like us, shepherd-people, hurry off to him who was once lying in a manger. It still matters that you take the light of Christ with you in your attitude, activities, words, and in your smile. It still matters that there is rejoicing in heaven over one sinner who repents through the message of the messenger, and to remember that you may be the loving messenger sent with that good news. It still matters that God's people know that they are kings and priests cleansed by the great high priestly death and that they proclaim atonement full and free. It still matters that God's people do not overlook the neglected, the desolate, the forgotten, the multitasking busy people, the hurting, the searching, the dying, remembering that he "has lifted up the humble" (Luke 1:52). It still matters that "his mercy extends to those who fear him, from generation to generation" (verse 50), even to Generation X and Generation Y who need the engagement of the one in the manger and the listening, loving relationship of all who follow him.

> "We are the Church; Christ bids us show
> That in his Church all nations find
> Their hearth and home where Christ restores
> True peace, true love to humankind" (CW 518:5).[6]

Letters from a Counselor

In a December 5 editorial, Garrison Keillor wrote about his recent experience of teaching a teenage Sunday school class in a New York church. He said that some of them seemed to be on a faith journey away from the Nicene Creed, toward something cooler and more humorous. But the students let Keillor say his piece, after which they said their pieces, "and what shone through was a sensible anxiety about the future and the fact that they care a lot about each other." But Keillor described his piece, the Nativity, as "the magical story [that is the] cornerstone of the Christian faith.... Without the Nativity, we become a sort of lecture series and coffee club, with not very good coffee and sort of aimless lectures. On Christmas Eve...we stand in the dimness and sing about the silent holy night and tears come to our eyes and the vast invisible forces of Christmas stir in the world. Skeptics, stand back. Hush. Hark. There is much in this world that doubt cannot explain.... A day in New York can show you such startling sights, including a band of doubting teenagers clustered in church on a snowy morning, that the birth of the child in the hay seems not so impossible after all, even appropriate, *even necessary.*"[7]

**"Softly from his lowly manger Jesus calls one and all,
'You are safe from danger.
Children, from the sins that grieve you, you are freed;
All you need I will surely give you'" (CW 37:5).**

Today many, especially the young, have a deep anxiety about the future, even while they care about each

Christ to the World with Joy We Bring

other. What screams to be invited directly into the center of that picture is the Christ of the manger, the cross, and the resurrection grave, the one in whom all things hold together. This season still does matter, even with all its busyness in your life and in the life of your church. The lights you put up, Christmas for Kids, Advent by Candlelight, special worship promoted by 5X7-inch cards, messages of peace in Christ—all become part of a national consciousness toward deeper things. Maybe even a skeptic will be caused to hush, to hark. The message of the nativity is that engaging, that connecting, that potent. Even angels were moved to sing about it. Let them continue their praise through you this season and next year!

This message goes to a variety of people in many situations. In Christ, Anita joins me in our love, delight, and prayers of thanks to God for you and what you do all year long. Who knows what the impact will be when...

"Christ to the world with joy we bring" (CW 518:1).

Wayne Schulz,
Mission Counselor
Christmas 2007

Holy Week 2008

St. Patrick and Holy Week 2008

It seems strange that a Lutheran would even mention St. Patrick at this sacred time of the church year. This is the only time in my lifetime, I am told, that St. Patrick's Day will occur during Holy Week. So he merits a little scrutiny, not so much to praise him but to thank God who used him as a mighty instrument to bring the message of Jesus to the people of Ireland. In the little research that I have done on the words of St. Patrick, what stick out are humility, urgency, energy, faithfulness, and a burning desire to share Jesus with the precious souls of Ireland.

> We ought to fish well and with diligent care, as the Lord commands and teaches, saying, "Follow me, and I will make you fishers of men." This is why it was most necessary to spread our nets widely so that a great throng and multitude might be captured for

God.... As Jesus says, "This gospel of the kingdom shall be preached in the entire world for a testimony to all races of people, and then shall the end come."

...That is why, never wearied, I tirelessly give thanks to my God.... So whatever happens to me, good or evil, I must accept readily and always give thanks to God, who has taught me to believe in him always without hesitation....

This is how the people of Ireland, who had never had any knowledge of God, but until now had cults and worshiped idols and abominations, have lately been turned into the people of the Lord and are called the children of God.[8]

When reading Patrick's intense and almost Pauline-type of internal urgency to love and reach Ireland's lost people, one can feel somewhat insignificant and certainly lukewarm in comparison. Lukewarm makes God sick (Revelation 3:16).

It's time for repentance when we don't see a crying need to reach the people in the areas in which God has placed us. It's time for repentance when we disregard a new generation among which 1 in 5 say they have essentially no faith—that used to be 1 in 20. It's time for repentance when outsiders have come to the impression that Christians are not genuinely interested in others. It's time for repentance when love for God and love for our neighbors are not foremost in our everyday lives, thoughts,

St. Patrick and Holy Week 2008

plans, and actions. It is time for repentance when we think GREEN will save the world.

Holy Week is not about St. Patrick. It is about Jesus. Take a close look at him, teaching and loving to the very end. Take a close look at Jesus crucified and dead. Take a close look at Jesus rising from the grave, alive, appearing to many, and proclaiming himself as resurrection and life. How we need Jesus! His good news changed Patrick. His good news delights and changes us to be his lights forever. Thanks be to God!

We children of light have enough mission statements. What we need are mission involvement and missional relationships. The living Savior moves us to get out of bed, out of the pews, out of our doors, out of our shells. Wear the gospel, rejoice in the gospel, live the gospel, and proclaim the gospel.

There are so many Patrick-like people we work with and have come to appreciate. Some come and go from subsidized mission congregations. All are gifts from God. I single out one because he has served all of us in Home Missions for a good number of years. He has trained and sent thousands of young people to assist mission congregations in their work of outreach and evangelism. He helped pick up pieces and people in New York City after 9/11 and in New Orleans after Katrina. He has been on other rescue missions and served as an inspiration to many. He has certainly been a team player with all of us in advancing the message of Jesus. I speak of Rich Warnecke who is leaving WELS Kingdom Workers for outreach work in a parish. Thanks, Rich, and may your future ministries be blessed in Pewaukee.

That leads me to the reminder that any mission-minded congregation can request manpower help for outreach and follow-up through the Faith in Action program of WELS Kingdom Workers. It is time to plan now for any request for the calendar year 2009. All requests have to go through district mission boards in August for approval by the Board for Home Missions in September. Forms are available on the WELS Kingdom Workers Web site.

> But I pray that...whoever discovers this document and reads these words, composed in Ireland by an unlearned sinner named Patrick—let no one ever say that what little I have accomplished was the work of this ignorant man alone. No, rather, know this and believe this: that it was a gift from God, that it occurred only for God's reasons. And that is my confession before I die.[9]

We give thanks for those who have gone before us, who have shared with us and others God's good news in Christ. May we march forward in similar love and zeal to bring the gospel to capture a large audience in 2008.

Fish well and with diligent care in the name of the risen Christ!
Wayne Schulz

Christmas 2008

When's It Going to Happen?

"Wachet auf! Wake, awake, for night is flying." The first four songs on my new Christmas CD from Trinity College, Cambridge, are renditions of "Sleepers, Awake." We Lutherans own that song. Its haunting message stirs the soul. We sing it with earnest urgency year after year. Perhaps all too often just to ourselves? An overview of 2008 arouses the need for all people everywhere to "Wake, awake."

There is urgency in the plea from God to his people. "Now is the time of God's favor, now is the day of salvation" (2 Corinthians 6:2). Yet do we sit in a sleepy trance, as though everything will soon get better? As though we take Christmas, Easter, Ascension, and Pentecost for granted? As though Advent is just a sentimental pre-Christmas period? I love the seasons of the church year. In reality, all of life until the Lord returns is an Advent season, a time to "Wake, awake." We need a daily dose of preparedness and preparing until the King returns and turns our mourning into dancing. Then even the trees of the field will clap their hands.

Where is our Advent urgency?

A non-Lutheran pleads, "Where are you Lutherans today at this stage of history? With your rich theological and worship heritage, with your history of bringing to all the world the Reformation's message of salvation by God's grace, why aren't you up front today in finding ways to communicate and bring Jesus to our floundering postmodern culture? Where are you today?"

A video depicts a forlorn 20-something addressing all of us sitting comfortably in our churches. She asks, "So, when's it going to happen? What are you going to do when you leave that building? When are you going to tell me about this person you follow, this person who makes a difference in your life? When are you going to show me what unconditional love looks like? When's it going to happen?" Desperate urgency. Sometimes it is hidden or disguised. But it's all around us if we do any observing or listening at all. Does it tug at the heart?

Song of the Baptist

With Advent urgency I attended the seminary's Christmas concert and heard once again the grand and uplifting themes in the songs of the saints and angels. Even

When's It Going to Happen?

there in the concert's center came penetrating questions from the haunting voice of today's John the Baptist:

> "Who will live this man's repentance?
> Who will walk his stony way?
> Who will leave their hurt behind them?
> Who will greet the dawning day?
> *Who will dare shake up the people?*
> *Who will speak for silent tongues?*
> Who will share the greatest mystery:
> God redeems us in his Son?"[10]

Once again the forlorn groans of a desperate world ask God's people, "When's it going to happen? When are you going to look at me, talk to me, tell me about that person who is so important to you?" It's always Advent, always time to ponder urgency, always time to reflect on God's Christmas grace in the setting of the Incarnation. Now it's time to pay attention to the world's wailing cry in the midst of its woes and financial failures. Especially for us with our rich heritage, for us to whom the Lord has given much, for us who know with certainty, "While all things were in quiet silence, and night was in the midst of her swift course, thine almighty Word, O Lord, leaped down out of thy royal throne. Alleluia."[11]

In the midst of night's swift course, are we distracted?

Letters from a Counselor

Home Missions was regaining some momentum this year. Renewed energy filled the room. Planning was progressive, at least according to our standards. The word was going out. Requests were being readied. Now, instead of advancement, there is talk about scaling back, retrenching. Financial woes distract, sometimes even from the Lord's mission. Corporate Christianity can't do it all alone. We no longer have the luxury of sitting back and watching others do it, even as we scrutinize their every step. Our Advent King teaches us that once again.

The world of wailing woes can still be reached with ministry enhancements in congregations and through renewed efforts by mission-minded people like you. You best can serve in the area where you are positioned, where there certainly are people who wonder, "When's it going to happen?" It will happen when the Lord's love leads you to an audience to work with his urgent cry, "Come to me!" As you approach 2009, it will be good to put the question in bold print in your meeting rooms, in your office, at the church doors, and in your heart, "When's it going to happen?" Add to that the picture of a woman who wrote to a Chicago newspaper, "I've often felt that I'm standing outside looking through the window of a party to which I was not invited."

It can begin in simplicity with the invitation of the Christmas carol of my childhood:

When's It Going to Happen?

"Come hither, ye children, O come one and all,
To Bethlehem haste, to the manger so small;
God's Son for a gift has been sent you this night
To be your Redeemer, your joy and delight."

Thank you for all your efforts in 2008. Wake, awake for renewed inviting efforts in 2009!

Anita joins me in wishing you, your family, your loved ones, and your congregation Advent, Christmas, and New Year's greetings as you celebrate your God-given and mission-minded life in Jesus.

Wayne Schulz
Mission Counselor
December 2008

Holy Week 2009

What Shall I Do with Christ?

It is the Palm Sunday scene as I write, children with palm branches, enthusiastic singing, a message to fit the remembrance of this day. One is tempted to jump immediately to Easter, the resurrection of the Christ, and to join the burning hearts of the Emmaus disciples as they reflect on what the victorious Jesus told them when he opened the Scriptures. But don't rush to the victory celebration.

First, there is Maundy Thursday, the institution of the life-giving meal, the command to love one another, the example that washed the feet of fickle friends who ran away naked and left Jesus to his enemies—alone. Second, there is Friday, oddly called good, with "Christ, the Death of death, our foe, who, thyself for me once giving to the darkest depths of woe" (CW 114:1). Stay awhile with this dark day which breaks your heart with all its cruelty and hatred. Do not shun this darkness if you expect to appreciate the light of the Easter conquest. This week is the center upon which the universe turns. In this week's killing, which some call senseless, we are brought to our senses. This week makes every individual ask with Pilate, "What shall I do, then, with Jesus who is called Christ?" (Matthew 27:22).

What shall I do with Christ? "Follow me," he says to all. It is through life in his cross that we find truth and value and purpose in all we do. This life we live in a distant country until we through Christ come home to our waiting Father.

And so we listen to Jesus say from that cross, "Father, forgive them." We may think, "So many bad and monstrous people throughout history have needed to hear that. In comparison, all I need is a forgiving wink from an understanding God." Someone has said it so well, "To belittle our sins is to belittle their forgiveness, to belittle the love of the Father who welcomes us home. Only he can bring us home who comes from home, who comes from God." So we look forward to Easter, God from God rising from the dead, "the firstfruits of those who have fallen asleep" (1 Corinthians 15:20). Our comfort is this, "For as in Adam all die, so in Christ all will be made alive" (1 Corinthians 15:22). As homebound saints we rejoice and give thanks. Then we heed the word of St. Paul, "Always

What Shall I Do With Christ?

give yourselves fully to the work of the Lord" (1 Corinthians 15:58).

"What shall I do, then, with Christ?" Direct that question to those you meet with all their baggage in their real and lonely world. They must know that they are saved not by their record, but by the record of Christ who came to love, to serve, to die, to rise again—to save, to call and bring lost people home. We know the theological facts. May God use this week to bring us to a fuller understanding of the good news of Jesus, to live it, and to share it as often as possible. May our hearts burn within us as the Scriptures are opened and we hear the cry of our Savior, "Follow me."

We have many distractions at this time in our church body as we also feel repercussions from our national recession. Many are concerned about our worker-training schools and the return of world missionaries. Many will also be shocked to hear that home missionaries are in the same boat of wondering about their future service. Personally, I have not seen anything like this in all my years in home missions.

My encouragement to you under the cross of Jesus is to pray as never before, to think and brainstorm with your people as never before, and to ask as never before, "What shall we do with Jesus who is called Christ?" How can we take the Jesus of this Holy Week to as many as possible so that all in the area we serve can hear his call to follow him? In the good news of God's promises to his people, I am confident that God can open doors of new opportunities when his forgiven people are listening, studying, thinking, praying, and acting according to his Word. Think of all the possibilities! Self-pity and worry sessions will help no one.

You can help spread the news of how the gospel is marching forward into people's hearts through your ministries. We need stories for *Mission Connection* and the WELS Mission Blog. They can be short *or* as long as 450 words. Interesting photos also help to make the story come alive. Please send articles and ideas to me as soon as you can. For *Mission Connection,* I need the stories *by April 16.* As of today, I have no stories for the next issue. So, please help spread the word.

I will end with a note to missionaries and boards in the Western Wisconsin, Northern Wisconsin, Southeastern Wisconsin, and Minnesota Districts. We feel at this time that it is essential to have our *missionaries' conference* as in past years. We will meet at Wisconsin Dells on October 26 and 27. Please mark the dates on your calendars.

Yours in Christ,
Wayne Schulz
Mission Counselor

Christmas 2009

Your Life Is Not Insignificant

*"Little children, can you tell?
Do you know the story well?"*

This is not a letter to little children. But its hope is to inspire you to tell children and those of all generations the story that they may or may not have heard, the meaning of the story they may or may not know. To do that we bow in humility at the manger of Jesus, kiss the ground before his feet, and stare in wonder and amazement as we ponder the Incarnation.

It is refreshing that a scribe in faith has daubed the Incarnation as the most shocking doctrine of Christianity. It is the *Magnum Mysterium* about which hymn writers have mused and musicians have composed. Even the Nicene Creed does not explain but describes and paints a picture of pointed truth and amazement at the event, "God from God, Light from Light, true God from true God.... Incarnate of the Holy Spirit and the virgin Mary, and became fully human."

"How can this be?" is a question that turns our minds to the love and wisdom of God. "Why did this occur?" is the real question. Here the Creed answers clearly as it points to our broken hearts and lives and any arrogance that may still lurk there:

For us and for our salvation, he came down from heaven.

Only those who make God too small can walk away from this scene disconcertedly and unamazed. How can we approach them in the same kind of concerned love with which God loved us by sending Jesus in his amazing Incarnation? Can our hearts go out to the unamazed, all who need a change in connection—a pull away from attachment to their flesh and the tendency to wander through life aimlessly and carelessly? Can we listen more actively to many who say, "Things are OK," when in essence their lives are connected to empty promises of wealth and power and physical security? The casual "Things are OK" is often a lie cleverly covered up. Without Incarnation and all that followed, things are not OK—nothing is OK. Without connection to Jesus, nothing is OK—for anyone.

"In him all things hold together" (Colossians 1:17).

Your Life is Not Insignificant

Without our effort or choosing, God in love connected with us on earth. As the down payment of that deep love, he sent Jesus in Incarnation. Willing obedience, crucifixion, resurrection, and ascension followed—the cornerstones of Christianity and our faith, features of his grace, and full payment for our sins, failures, and nagging frustrations with ourselves and others. It is difficult to keep all of that out of the Incarnation. Nor should we. Everything works together and holds together in the Incarnate Christ. We have every reason for celebration. So celebrate delightfully and, like little children, gather joyfully at the manger.

> "With pounding heart I stare:
> a child, a son, the Prince of Peace for me,...
> To die, to live, and not alone for me,
> To die, to live, AND NOT ALONE FOR ME" (CW 54:3,4).

In his manger hymn, Martin Luther says something that amazes even further:

> "Be of good cheer and let no sorrow move you.
> For God's own child in mercy mild *joins you to him*—
> how greatly God must love you!" (CW 40:3).

Move on to the continuing part and heart of Incarnation. The Incarnation of Jesus is God's saving connection to his earth's people. Jesus, the One who was, and is, and is to come **is still fully God and fully human.** In undeserved and shocking truth he connects with you and is joined to you in gospel, in baptism, in bread and wine of the Lord's Supper. We talk so much about him, sometimes, even somewhat arrogantly in our weaker moments, without truly appreciating and sensing his presence—right now. **"I am with you always,"** says the Lord of Incarnation, resurrection, and ascension. With St. Paul you have every right to speak, and live, and have your being in "Christ who lives in me." Here and now, even while you and all the little children stare at the manger, you can also say and sing with confidence, "Christ is born and he is here—now." Remember it in joy and confidence when you preach, when you witness, when you publish, and especially when you demonstrate in your everyday life the Christ who lives in you. Jesus says, "All these Scriptures—they point to me." Our job as we walk around and away from the manger is to bring Jesus of the Scriptures and of Incarnation to his people, people who journey with us through this God-loved world, people who still have to come to know that they are loved beyond comprehension, people who are still skeptics and not sure about anything. Go to them. Find them. Into their vacuum comes Incarnation, with God using you as his tool to represent him, to imitate him in serving love, to tell of the depth of that forgiving love.

"For in Christ all the fullness of the Deity lives in bodily form, and you have been given fullness in Christ, who is the head over every power and authority" (Colossians 2:9,10).

Your Life is Not Insignificant

Your life is not insignificant as you proclaim and serve your Savior, as you elevate thoughts to an understanding of what it means to be of Christ and in Christ and for the Christ whose entire ministry was for you and others. It is in the contemplation of his grace that the Holy Spirit humbles you deeply and elevates you powerfully to all the possibilities that fullness in Christ gives you in life. This means not despising those who still do not know Jesus. It also means not being intimidated by anyone, because the Incarnate Christ was given as the good news of great joy for you and everyone you meet, even the little children and others who may not yet know the story well that Jesus is the radiance of God's glory.

God's gifted people, like you, amaze me. Your growth in Jesus, your ministry efforts, your mission zeal, and your witness are noticed, appreciated, and prayed for. With the fullness of Christ, love and serve those around you, your family, your congregation, your community where God has placed you, wherever you have opportunity to gain an audience for the good news of the Savior. Anita joins me in prayer that your home's Christmas and your lives are blessed and a blessing to many through the Incarnate Christ, Immanuel—God with us.

Wayne Schulz,
Mission Counselor

Holy Week 2010

Easter Words

"Children of God, dying and rising,
Sing to the Lord a new song!
Heaven and earth, hosts everlasting,
Sing to the Lord a new song!
He has done marvelous things.
I, too, will praise him with a new song!"[12]

Herbert Brokering, hymn writer, book author, and Luther scholar now stands in joy beside his Savior. I once met this man at one of his workshops and remember him as one who was alive in Jesus, alive to God's people, and one who delighted in all of God's creation, seen or unseen. He had a passion for words and often gave single words as baptismal presents to children. He connected words with the Word becoming flesh and fresh in Jesus. His writing evoked a childlike joy and faith in Jesus and all he has done.

Brokering also wrote little parables which were interesting to use as spiritual discussion starters with youth groups. Here is one. *"There once was a church where there were many scientists. Their minister was once a scientist. He never has candles on the altar. He always has Bunsen burners. All the scientists have the feeling that their lab tables are like altars, and they all have a candle in their lab. The minister never told them to do it. They decided this on their own. No one ever asked them what it means."* What are some of the themes of Christian life and vocation in this parable? What concern does the last sentence evoke?

This is Holy Week, when all of us proclaim and hear familiar words, words that have transforming power and impact in the lives of everyone. This year I leave you with a few Easter words and phrases that we often speak rapidly or hear in their context. Standing alone in their innocence, these and many others reach out to us and surprise us when we think about them and place ourselves into the resurrection scenario.

- *Early*…while it was still *dark*.
- His appearance was like *lightning*.
- In their *fright* the women *bowed* down with their faces to the ground.
- *Why* seek ye the *living* among the dead? (an evangelism tool with dozens of illustrations)

Easter Words

- He is *not here;* he is *risen.*
- They did not believe the women because their *words seemed* to them *like nonsense.*
- Both were *running.*
- The cloth was *folded.*
- They *still* did not understand the scripture that Jesus *had* to rise from the dead.
- Woman, *why* are you crying? *Who is it you are looking for?*
- She saw Jesus *standing* there.
- Mary.
- Rabboni!
- Do not *hold on* to me.
- I am *returning* to *my* Father and *your* Father.
- The doors *locked.*
- *Peace* be with you.
- As the Father sent me, I am *sending you.*
- My Lord and *my God!*
- How *foolish* you are and how slow of heart to believe all that the prophets have spoken.
- *Stay* with us, for it is evening; the <u>day is</u> *almost over.* (What a day!)
- *He took bread,* gave thanks, broke it.
- *Then* their *eyes* were *opened.*
- And he *disappeared* from their sight.
- Were not our hearts *burning* within us?
- Jesus *stood* among them and said, *Peace* be with you.
- *Friends,* haven't you any *fish?*
- Do you have *anything* here *to eat?*

Letters from a Counselor

- Repentance and forgiveness of sins will be preached in his name *to all nations.*
- *You* are *witnesses* of these things.

Resurrection surprises! The King of kings lives, stands among us as Savior, knows us by name, is interested in the food on our tables, sends away our fears about the present and the future, and is definitive that his mission to let the world know all this continues through us until he returns or we return to him.

This will be my last Holy Week message to you, at least as mission counselor. As of the end of June, I will retire from the mission counselor position, but not from Christianity, from proclamation, or from friends. Over the last 20 years I have been privileged to work with a multitude of missionaries, mission board members and chairmen, many other colleagues and friends, and helpful people like Harry Hagedorn and Mel Schuler. Thank you, Jesus, for all of you!

As we go out resurrectionizing the world, we remember Brokering's prayer for each of us:

Lord, send me a surprise. One that catches me off guard and makes me wonder…like Easter.
Send me a resurrection when everything looks dead and buried.
Send me light when night seems too long.
Send me spring when the cold and frozen season seems endless.
Send me an idea when my mind is empty.

Easter Words

Send me a thing to do when I am just waiting around.
Send me a new friend when I am alone.
Send me peace when I am afraid.
Send me a future when it looks hopeless.
Send me your Resurrection when I die, Jesus!

>Yours in Jesus,
>Wayne Schulz
>Mission Counselor

CHRISTMAS 2010

BOLD IN THE FAITH

Dear missionaries and mission-minded friends. In front of me is a multi-paged Christmas letter. Though well-intended, it makes no mention of Jesus. While promoting Lutheran orthodoxy, it also assails those who are somewhat less than orthodox. The claim of orthodoxy with no mention of Jesus has the hollow sound of arrogance in it. It brings no one to their knees, does not show the way to Paradise, converts no one to follower-ship of Jesus. It does not echo the spirit of Mary who said, **"My spirit rejoices in God my Savior, for he has been mindful of the humble state of his servant"** (Luke 1:47,48).

Martin Franzmann says that in the Magnificat (Luke 1:46-55), Mary "sings of the God who, *holy* and *mighty*, has in mercy condescended to make her the object and instrument of his redeeming work. The vocabulary of her faith is the vocabulary of the OT, the Song of Hannah (1 Samuel 2:1-10) and the doxological language of the Psalms and prophets.... She sees in her own history the continuation of the story of the divine *mercy* which *is on those who fear their God and Savior* (v. 50); more than that, she sees that story drawing to its triumphant close; she sees the dawn of the final fulfillment of all God's promises to his people (v.55). That final triumph is, for her faith, so certain that she speaks of it (as also many OT prophets did) as already accomplished; God HAS triumphed in his sovereign mercy to *those of low degree,* to the *hungry;* while the *proud,* the *mighty,* and the *rich,* the self-assertive men who feel no need of his mercy and refuse it, are overridden and destroyed. *The blessing promised to Abraham* (Genesis 12:1-3) for all the families of the earth *is breaking forth to do its work in all the earth;* in the face of God's gracious action all human standards of greatness are inverted, all human greatness melts away."[13] (This quote captures the spirit of Christianity.)

Recently a Luther scholar surmised that Luther would simply say "Jesus" when asked how he would answer the question, "What is Christianity about?" We followers of Luther live in a well-storied life with the whole of the Scriptures being our well-source. We cannot live our Christianity without these stories of good news that God brought to the earth when he sent Jesus, our Immanuel, our "God with us." What stories of Jesus and his love do you like to tell whether you are sermonizing, sharing, or reflecting on your faith? What makes your heart and life tick? What makes you bold in the faith? There is a world out there longing to hear your story, the story of how the good news of Jesus makes all the difference in all of life and throughout eternity. That is a story of forgiveness and an eternal future in the splendor of God. It is the story that makes your spirit also rejoice in God as your Savior.

Jesus is the good news that descended from on high to make all the difference for all the world. Everyone in the world, everyone in that part of the world where you serve, whether admitting it or not, is looking for the way to peace, security, well-being, total satisfaction. No matter what they call it, it is the desire to get back to the tree of life in God's perfect garden called Eden. But God keeps us away from that physical place and asks us to look to another tree instead, the tree of the cross of Jesus and all it stands for, our passageway to the Tree of Life described in the last chapter of God's final book in the Bible. So, how do we get there? Jesus came to tell us so simply, **"I am the way and the truth and the life"** (John 14:6). There is the simple and comforting answer, one that saves from despair over sin and failures, the answer that has the authority of Immanuel, God with us, behind it.

The Christ Child we celebrate this Advent/Christmas season is also the one who issues the call to discipleship: *"Follow me."* Why follow Jesus? Because he says, *"I am the way."* There are books by the dozen about *leadership* in the church. And all of you are leaders in one way or another. The Bible says much about faithfulness with the gospel in leadership. But it also says much about follower-ship. Leadership flows out of follower-ship or discipleship. The more we know about Jesus is not a ticket to lead us to arrogance, but as in the life of Mary, a reminder to ponder these things in our hearts. And then to speak and sing of them, to tell the story of Jesus. Great leadership flows from thorough follower-ship, being in, with, and under Jesus. And so we kneel at the manger and its message again this Christmas season. The miracle of the Incarnation reminds us of how little we know about the depths of God's love. Or, as someone put it in a theological journal, "We know precious little about God, but the little we know is precious."

I greet you no longer in an official capacity, but as one who prays for you and has a heart for what God has called you to do. I greet you as people in whom God dwells and through whom he breaks forth to do his work in all the earth. All this, through the stories of Jesus that are in your heart and life, the Christmas story of his Advent that sets you, his people, free, free to believe and rejoice, free to bring Jesus to others.

Anita joins me in greeting you and extending God's blessings to you and your families for your Christmas celebration and New Year. Please continue to send us reports of the forward march of the gospel so that we know how to pray and give thanks for you!

Bold in the Faith

Yours in the Christ of Bethlehem,
Wayne Schulz
Mission Counselor — retired

Holy Week 2011

Rejoicing in the Resurrection Grave

People are not just to be noticed, looked at, or halfheartedly listened to. Is "I see you—notice, honor, hear, and understand you" a practiced part of your life? Observe a few examples from Jesus in ministry.

There is *Zacchaeus*, short, sitting in a tree, yet not invisible to Jesus. "Zacchaeus, come down immediately. I must stay at your house today." No appointment. No texting. No "When you come to church, I will visit you," but personal, pointed, and immediate attention. At once Zacchaeus came down and welcomed Jesus gladly. To Jesus there was urgency, followed by meaningful conversation over dinner and proclamation of his ministry plan. "For the Son of Man came to seek and to save what was lost" (Luke 19:10).

Letters from a Counselor

Lazarus was dead, much to the chagrin of Mary and Martha, close friends of Jesus. In a move that would startle the people of that day, Jesus went to the grave of Lazarus and cried, "Lazarus, come out!" (John 11:43). Notice that even the dead hear his voice. Much power accompanies the voice of Jesus. Something to think about for your future this week. "For since death came through a man, the resurrection of the dead comes also through a man. For as in Adam all die, so in Christ all will be made alive" (1 Corinthians 15:21,22).

Think of *Judas* in the events of this week. A failed disciple, yet not dismissed by Jesus even at the height of his betrayal. "Judas, are you betraying the Son of Man with a kiss?" (Luke 22:48). "Friend, do what you came for" (Matthew 26:50). Jesus cared for Judas even while Judas carried out his deplorable activity.

At the scene of the empty tomb in Joseph's garden, *Mary* was crying. Not realizing that the risen Jesus, the second Adam, was standing there; and, thinking he was the gardener (reminiscent of the first Adam, Eden's gardener), she told him, "Tell me where you have put him." To which Jesus responded by saying to her, "Mary." What a difference that made in her moment, her perception, her life.

Jesus gave Mary an assignment. "Go...to my *brothers* and tell them, 'I am returning to my Father and your Father, to my God and your God'" (John 20:17). Note

Rejoicing in the Resurrection Grave

that Jesus calls men who had forsaken and denied him his brothers.

These and many other references display that in Jesus there is a passionate heart that has saving love and personal concern for people. The resurrection of Jesus is the event that changed the world and its history. It opens the Holy Scriptures and cracks the shell of human hearts. The proclamation of the resurrection of our Lord draws people to Christ, reorders Christian lives, builds the church, and awakens you to the truth that Jesus knows your name, too, and in him you will live, really live.

In the midst of all the glory of Jesus' resurrection morning, there is a power at work in your responsive heart toward love, concern, and compassion for a world of bruised and beaten people. For years most of us have heard and deemed the resurrection to be the greatest news of all time. We are moved to say, "Did not our hearts burn within us while Jesus walked with us and opened the Scriptures for us?" The greatest message deserves the greatest efforts at promoting it, for it is all centered in the Redeemer Christ who lives, who calls us by name. We are his!

As you journey through life among bruised and beaten people, take note of them. People boxed in hospitals or clinic waiting rooms. People wandering aimlessly through grocery stores. People feeling pains of separation and aloneness even at wedding celebrations. People looking lost in church building gathering areas. People texting endlessly in airports or other public areas. Be bold and connect with them. You have a story for them about the Savior-God who knows them by name. Christian being is also a way of Christian acting. Christians care about the things that Jesus directs them to care about: serving the hurting, loving the lost, and proclaiming to people the risen Jesus.

Connecting with people comes at a high price to your personal convenience and habits. It means focusing on an individual as Jesus did. When you divide your attention between the person in front of you while giving snippets of digital attention to someone else, it is disrespectful, annoying, and makes people feel invisible. Digital attention can be good; just so the individual is not lost in the haste of your multitasking.

As you, servants of the Savior's selfless love, go about your work, stay fascinated with people. Each person is unique and an individual. Each person is part of the general yet specific message that in Christ God so loved "the world." You walk in your part of God's world each day. What a splendid place that is! And what groups of people and individuals there are who need to hear that life is more than politics and money and friendships and fleeting forms of entertainment. Life is special and filled with peace and purpose and joy in Jesus. No box or rocky cave could hold him. He lives! You need to know and

Rejoicing in the Resurrection Grave

rejoice in this truth of a completed plan of salvation, even as you are compelled to tell about it.

Rejoicing with you in the message of the resurrection grave!

Wayne Schulz

[signature]

Afterword

October 8, 2011

Heaven has a new soul who just arrived tonight....a soul rejoicing "in the message of that resurrection grave" he wrote about just a few months earlier.

Dad has now taken his place with the rest of the saints in heaven, rejoicing in being in God's presence and praising God for all the amazing love he has shown us through his Son, Jesus. This day was a huge victory celebration on earth and heaven because this faithful follower of Christ finished his race and is now enjoying a new and perfect life in the presence of God and all his angels. A victory celebration because of Jesus' resurrection!

> "Hallelujah! For our Lord God Almighty reigns!
> Let us rejoice and be glad and give him glory!
> For the wedding of the Lamb has come,
> and his bride had made herself ready....
> Blessed are those who are invited to
> the wedding supper of the Lamb!"
> (Revelation 19:6-9).

My family will miss Dad.

But we aren't the only ones. He touched the lives of many people.

Dad spent his life preaching and teaching and proclaiming Christ. The one thing that mattered most to him was the mission of spreading this good news to everyone in the world. And helping churches do that very thing. Now he is enjoying and living that good news. Now he is experiencing the thing that he has been so excitedly telling people about all his life. I look forward to seeing him again. I imagine you do, too. Thanks to Jesus, we don't have to say good-bye. We told him, "We'll see you in heaven."

For me, I have never been more excited to worship God and praise him for what he has made possible for every one of us—eternal life through Jesus. I am looking forward to joining every one of you in offering up to God a true thanksgiving as we worship him, whether we are together or in our own congregations.

Afterword

If there is one thing, one truth, this event has strengthened me in, it is this:

Jesus is the only thing that matters.

We worship a living Savior. Nothing else matters!
Joel Schulz
October 8, 2011

NOTES

My father was a well-read man. He spent a lot of time learning and growing, as he read everything from ancient works to the latest books published on church and ministry. He wasn't writing these letters with the intent of publishing them, so they didn't come with footnotes for all of his sources. We have attempted to do the best job we could do to track down every source and give credit where credit is due. But it is entirely possible that there are thoughts and ideas from his reading that wound up in these letters that we weren't aware of or weren't able to track. So if he borrowed a deep thought or a line of poetry from you, and we didn't give you credit, please forgive us. We are indebted to you for the inspiration you gave him to write these letters for us.

Letters from a Counselor

[1] Mark Paustian, "The Iconoclast," *Forward in Christ,* Vol. 85, No. 12 (December 1998).

[2] *Christian Worship: Occasional Services* (Milwaukee: Northwestern Publishing House, 2004), p. 200.

[3] Colleen Carroll, *The New Faithful—Why Young Adults Are Embracing Christian Orthodoxy* (Chicago: Loyola Press, 2002), p. 3.

[4] Cranach: The Blog of Veith, December 14, 2006, www.geneveith.com/archives-from-old-site-2006/ (accessed November 11, 2012).

[5] First Things, December 1993, www.firstthings.com/onthesquare/2006/12/bottum-ps-christmases-past (accessed November 11, 2012).

[6] James Quinn, "Forth in the Peace of Christ We Go," © 1969 James Quinn. Admin. by Continuum International Publishing Group. Used by permission.

[7] A Prairie Home Companion, "The Nativity in New York City," December 4, 2007, prairiehome.publicradio.org/features/deskofgk/2007/12/11.shtml (accessed November 11, 2012).

NOTES

⁸ Greg Tobin, *The Wisdom of St. Patrick—Inspiration from the Patron Saint of Ireland* (New York: Fall River Press, 1999), pp. 115, 185-186, 211.

⁹ Greg Tobin, *The Wisdom of St. Patrick*, p. 217.

¹⁰ Excerpt from "Song of the Baptist" by Francis Patrick O'Brien. Copyright © 2002 by GIA Publications, Inc. 7404 S. Mason Ave., Chicago, IL 60638, www.giamusic.com, 800.442.1358. All rights reserved. Used by permission.

¹¹ George Appleton, *The Oxford Book of Prayers* (New York: Oxford University Press, Inc.).

¹² Text: Herbert Brokering, "Earth and All Stars," © 1968 Augsburg Publishing House, admin. Augsburg Fortress. Reproduced by permission. All rights reserved.

¹³ Martin Franzmann, *Concordia Bible with Notes,* Second Edition (St. Louis, MO: Concordia Publishing House, 1971), p. 110.